WORSHIP
THE
KING

WORSHIP THE KING

HENRY KRIETE

DPI

DISCIPLESHIP
PUBLICATIONS
INTERNATIONAL

Worship the King

ISBN: 1-57782-131-9

Cover Design: Chad Crossland
Book Design: Corey Fisher

To my best friend and fellow-adventurer,

Marilyn Ruth Kriete—

Your love for God and those around you, your integrity and simplicity, have always humbled me. Your affection and friendship, loyalty and love, have always lifted me.

And to my beautiful, gifted, loving and outrageously funny kids,

Daniel Anil and Natassja Théophé—

You have deepened my belief in the goodness and grace of God.

CONTENTS

RULES OF ENGAGEMENT

Through the years, I have been a fan of *Star Trek* and other space adventures. I love it when preparations are made to jump to "warp speed." A course is laid in, systems are checked, and there is a dramatic pause before the captain intones, "Engage!" With a flash, the ship streaks off the screen in a blur of rainbow colors. Those in the special effects field must live for moments like this.

Closer to home, Larry Wood, with whom I work in the publishing ministry, is always reminding our management team of our need to "engage" an important or pressing concern that needs consideration. This usually involves something that we are aware of, but that merits more than cursory attention on our part.

Then, there is that very special moment when a boyfriend or girlfriend is transformed into a fiancé(e). Songs, poems and stories have been written to commemorate the "engagement." Elaborate plans and diamond rings are but demonstrations that a particular human relationship is about to take on more significance than any ot0her in the lives of these two people. Each knows with joy that they have finally found *the one*.

This is a book about worshiping God. Worship is a powerful word, one that "engages" our whole being as we respond to God's overtures to us. It involves wholehearted, passionate adoration of our Creator-Redeemer-Judge. In the Hebrew Scriptures, the word for worship is *shachah,* which means "to depress, bow down, prostrate." In ancient times, worship was expressed with the physical action of bowing, sometimes to the point of falling prostrate (see Genesis 17:3). In the New Testament, the Greek word for worship is *proskuneo,* "to kiss (the hand or the ground) toward," as in the oriental fashion of bowing prostrate upon the ground. Next in frequency is *sebomai,* which is "to venerate, reverence, hold in awe." Finally, there is *latreuo,* which carries the idea "to serve (religiously), offer gifts, worship God in the observance of the rites instituted for his worship."[1] True worship requires thoughtful, disciplined effort. It demands an engagement on our part that goes far beyond being passive or simply entertained.

As someone who has picked up this book, you almost certainly participate in a weekly activity called a worship service. Yet we who would be worshipers of God must ask ourselves several important questions: (1) Do we really worship the Almighty God during those times, or do we just observe an organized program? (2) Do we limit our worship of the everywhere-present God to that two-hour slot in our weekly schedule, or do we live a life of worship? (3) Is our public and private worship transforming? Does it bring us so tangibly into the presence of God that we are changed as a result?

History teaches that no matter how vital or flourishing a religious movement might be at its outset, it inevitably undergoes some degree of institutionalization that can rob it of its vitality. The resulting forms are often just shadows of what were once significant and meaningful expressions of the heart. Worshipers become ritualists. Participants become spectators.

How can we keep this from happening in our own lives? We must "engage" God with all our being. *Feeling* close to God is not enough if it isn't based on a true understanding that informs and illuminates our experiences. And *knowing about* God is not enough if it is removed from an emotional experience of the personal presence of God in day-to-day life.

It is remarkable that the revealed word of God points to a God who desires just such a relationship with us. He demands worship that engages our whole self—heart and mind, in spirit and in truth.

---

[1] *The International Standard Bible Encyclopedia,* 1939 ed., s.v. "Worship."

"Love the Lord your God with all your heart and with all your
soul and with all your mind and with all your strength."
(Mark 12:30)

"A time is coming and has now come when the true worshipers
will worship the Father in spirit and truth, for they are the kind
of worshipers the Father seeks. God is spirit, and his worshipers must worship in spirit and in truth." (John 4:23-24)

We cannot afford to ignore either our intellect or our emotions if we
hope to approach God in a meaningful way.

I am excited about the book that you hold in your hands. It is the fruit
of a life that exudes devotion to God. As we have journeyed together in the
writing of this book, I have often been amazed at Henry's heart and
intense passion for his God. It has become obvious to me that this is the
primary reason for the impact he has had in places like Canada, India and
several African countries, not to mention many parts of the United States.
His desire to experience closeness with God as well as his love for the truth
of the Bible permeates and pervades his every word. You cannot miss the
tenderness and affection Henry feels for his Savior and at the same time,
his reverence and awe for the Creator and Judge of the universe. His
writing lifts us above religious routines and helps us to view God with a
new sense of wonder. At the same time it challenges us to make practical
decisions that will enrich the spiritual journey and bring honor to God.

As we who want to be serious disciples of Jesus grow in number,
and as the realities of our own institutions become more pronounced,
we must be determined to avert the slow death of religious movements
of the past. We must keep alive a vital experience of God to pass on to
our children and to theirs. We must learn fresh ways to exalt our Lord
and our God. So prepare to engage. Strap yourself in. Come, let us
worship the King!

Kelly Petre
October 2000

ACKNOWLEDGMENTS

First I want to thank Kip McKean, not only for discipling me and appointing me an evangelist so many years ago, but for being the first man to introduce me to the greatness and glory of God and the holiness and awesomeness of his kingdom. My years in Boston were the most formative in my life, no exception.

I want to thank our congregation in Indianapolis and our staff for their support and love, and their response to the concepts in this book. In particular, I am grateful for my fellow evangelists and their wives, Mark and Carol Morris and Steve and Tresene Cannon, among the dearest friends that I've ever had in the kingdom. And I also wish to acknowledge our worship leaders, Steve Cannon, Bill Culpepper and David Finnell.

I also want to thank Tom Jones and Mike Fontenot for believing in this project from the outset and encouraging me to put pen to paper.

Thanks to the entire staff at DPI, first for their spirit of love, then for their spirit of excellence. In particular I want to thank Chad Crossland and Corey Fisher for their design, and Kim Hanson and Vickie Boone for their extraordinary editorial help.

In Boston, I have a special band of prayer warriors who encouraged me so much during the writing of the book. Thanks to Vickie Boone, Robert Cataldo, Jeannine Loftus and Marc Perez, whose faithfulness in prayer, as much as anything, helped to pull this book together.

My love for science flourished while I lived in Arlington, Virginia. One big reason for that is because I had my own personal angel who worked in the Library of Congress, Deb Watts.

Others helped with input and typing and feedback, for which I am grateful: Katie Grotrian, Chris Hurst, Randy Anderson, Luanne Berk, Shari Finnell, Eleanor O'Brien and Kelly Lydon—who really is a member of our family.

11

I am grateful to Douglas Arthur and Larry Reed for their friendship and encouragement, and for allowing me the time and opportunity to write. I love both of you deeply.

I am deeply indebted to Mike Taliaferro, one of the greatest warriors in the kingdom, and one of the clearest and most gifted expositors of God's word that I know. His impact on my life and on my efforts and abilities as a teacher and preacher has been profound. In twenty-three years, I have never known a man who loves the Scriptures more.

And now, to the big three: A huge thank you goes out to Kelly Petre at DPI, who is not only an incredible editor but one who has a lyrical ear and deep love for God. His assistance has been invaluable, but I am especially grateful for the new friendship we have forged.

I want to thank Monica Hicks, who gave countless hours, at all hours of the day or night, and who was always joyful, always willing, always flexible. She typed or retyped, cut, pasted and arranged this manuscript two times. What a gift she and her husband, Lee, are to our church and especially to me.

And many thanks go to Marilyn, my wife—what a joy you are to me! Thank you for your patience and helpfulness over the last few months. You are a deeply faithful woman in prayer, in marriage and in ministry. It would have been impossible to write this or even feel as I do about worship without your partnership in Christ. If, by the grace of God, I am embraced in heaven, it is because you held my hand on earth.

Finally, my deepest thanks go out to my mom, Anna. Ever since my dad died, it is hard to put into words how much I cherish and need the love of my mom—a gentle and quiet spirit, always proud of me, the woman God chose to help me find him in my youth.

Not only is this a book about worship and of worship, but it was born of a desire to grow in worship. The joy and pleasure I received from God during the past few months have been overpowering at times. More than anything else, I hope these thoughts and words and scriptures inspire you to a recovery of wonder and worship as they have for me.

NEW WINE,
DEEPER WELLS

ISAAC REOPENED THE WELLS THAT HAD BEEN DUG IN THE
TIME OF HIS FATHER ABRAHAM.

GENESIS 26:18

WITH JOY YOU WILL DRAW WATER
FROM THE WELLS OF SALVATION.

ISAIAH 12:3

EVERYONE WAS FILLED WITH AWE.

ACTS 2:43

My study of worship began as a personal necessity. I clearly remember the Sunday last December when I vented my frustrations to God. I was organizing the worship service, but ironically I felt so preoccupied with the details that I couldn't seem to concentrate on God. In addition, with the holidays upon us, I had a ton of other stuff that I was anxious about. I recall sitting in the front row, an easy target for messages and notes and pieces of paper from Christians who were vying for my attention, even during the service. And on top of it all, I was sick to death of singing the same old songs! I had not gone there to truly worship and honor God that day, and so it may not surprise you that I did not leave church feeling rejuvenated. But it was my fault alone. I had allowed things to get away from me. I was anxious, not in awe; distracted, not devoted; bored, not bowled over. Like Martha, I was entangled in good things, but had forsaken the best. As a result, "worship" left me empty and frustrated—even a bit angry.

What I needed was to recover a sense of wonder. I needed to rediscover the privilege and joy of worship, to refocus on the basic elements of adoration, and to deepen my awe of God. I studied the Scriptures in earnest. I began to see worship with brand new eyes, as if God had opened them for the first time. From Genesis to Revelation, the primacy of worship, the need to worship, seemed overpowering. I began to recognize true and false worship *everywhere*—in the story of Cain and Abel, the patriarchs, the exodus and the decimation of Egypt; in the wanderings, the conquest of Canaan, the glory of law and temple worship and the reason for so much blood. I saw the place of worship in the psalms of David, the destruction of Jerusalem, the suffering of Job and the restoration of the temple; in the tearing down of idols, the judgment of kings and kingdoms; and in the announcement and birth of Jesus, his temptation and ministry, and in the motive and words of his brief life. Worship was part of the prelude to Pentecost, the sending out of missionaries from Antioch, the start and summation of every New Testament epistle, and it continued into the final glory of heaven. The theme of worship is everywhere, deeply embedded in every book, in almost every incident that took place in the Bible.

I am convinced that the greatest need in our churches—that which gripped us and launched our fledgling movement around the world in earlier days—is the sense of awe of God. We desperately need, particularly among more mature believers, a recovery of wonder, a deepening of awe, the new wine of true worship.

The reason many disciples turn away from God is because, in God's own words, "you forsake the LORD your God and have no awe of me" (Jeremiah 2:19). The reason so many disciples become spiritually tired, then entangled and overcome by the world is because our sense of awe has not only diminished, but vanished. And with that vanishing, we forfeit his divine blessing upon our worship. The reason disciples do not delight in and do not hunger for God's word is simple: We no longer "stand in awe of [God's] laws" (Psalm 119:120). And the reason many Christians are not willing to give their all for the Great Commission—

choosing instead to spend the best of themselves on their careers rather than the kingdom of God—is all too clear: We can no longer say with Habakkuk, "I stand in awe of your deeds" (Habakkuk 3:2). In short, if we are unable to "stand in awe of God," we will inevitably offer "the sacrifice of fools" (Ecclesiastes 5:1, 7), even fall away.

The answer to a stale or jaded heart, to cowardice or complacency, is to once again recover our awe of who God is, what he has done and what we are part of. We need to rekindle the sense of wonder we had as young disciples—the joy of our newfound salvation, the thrill of being a part of a powerful movement, the conviction that we belong to an invincible kingdom. We were "blown away" when we first experienced a depth of love in relationships that we never thought possible; the miracle of a completely integrated and interracial fellowship; the healing of broken families and the blessing of saved marriages. We had hearts that could be cut deeply by a Sunday sermon, cried tears after a cross study, and considered it a privilege to sell homes and cars and lands and horses and heirlooms for special missions contributions. The reason that many disciples—and sadly, even whole churches—have stopped growing and have become less radical, is because our sense of wonder and mystery, gratitude and love, has all but evaporated. We must allow God to break our hearts and to thrill us all over again; and once broken, we must at all costs guard against this kind of hardening ever happening again. Wonder, joy, surprise, spontaneity, faith, courage, deep sacrifice, numerical growth—these all flow from hearts in love and hearts in awe of God (see Acts 2:42-47). True worship proceeds from this kind of awe; and it is also, I believe, produced by this kind of awe.

Like Isaac, I needed to dig up and reopen the ancient wells of faith and worship (Genesis 26). And once again, I had to decide to drink deeply and joyfully "from the wells of salvation" (Isaiah 12:3). Thankfully, these wells never dry up. I believe it is time for all of us to return to their living waters. "Do not get drunk on wine," says Paul, but rather, be intoxicated with God's Spirit (Ephesians 5:18). The time has come for new wine and deeper wells, the heart and wonder and gift of worship.

THE GLORY OF
WORSHIP

Worship is the opportunity for busy people to touch the eternal, for sinners to glimpse the holy, for broken people to be enfolded in his perfect love. Worship is moving beyond our self-centered lives to meet the one who created us for something better.

Rob Frost

The chief end of man is to glorify God and to enjoy him forever.

The Westminster Catechism

We are called to adore and pay homage to God Almighty, and are privileged to be invited to do so; worship is thus an end in itself—indeed the highest of all ends. God seeks, and delights in, the praises of his people. Worship also serves to reorient us to the center of our existence and his will for our lives.

Donald Hustad

True worship is when the spirit, the immortal and invisible part of man, speaks to and meets with God, who is immortal and invisible.

William Barclay

Worship is written upon the heart of man by the hand of God...in a broad sense, worship is inseparable from and is an expression of life. It is not that man cannot live without worship, it is that he cannot *truly* live without worship...man was made to worship as surely as he was made to breath. We may restrict the expression of worship for a season, just as we may briefly hold our breath, but there is an inward craving for worship that cannot be permanently stilled.

Judson Cornwall

1

A Verb, a Kiss and a Knife

Worship is a verb—an act, a work. God reveals and we respond. We must be responsive. We cannot remain passive and think that we are worshiping. We do not gather for entertainment; God is not performing for us. It is God's prerogative to behold his creation and to be the observing audience—an audience of one. We are here to lift, to give, to exalt, to shout and to dance. As one of God's created beings, I am the donkey in this pageant, bearing a king and calling all creatures his praises to sing. If not me, then you. And if not us, then even "the stones will cry out" (Luke 19:40). And cry they will!

Worship is a kiss—a profusion of kissing, really, and a bowing at my Lord's feet with unfurled hair and tears. And amazingly, he kisses me too, with a kiss that proceeds from an infinite smile.

Worship is a knife—a bloody knife. I sacrifice my best, my whole being, even my firstborn, in honor of his life and his love. And I do this in reverence of his blood (see Genesis 22).

And finally, mysteriously, worship is hearing the distant sound of rolling thunder—the faint whisper across time that announces that something powerful is coming my way, that something wonderful, outrageously wonderful, is going to happen. This is worship.

Whether in public or in private, true worship is born from an intensely personal experience. True worship demands that we be fully engaged and that we do so with gusto and relish and awe. In worship we celebrate life, we long to taste mystery, and we desire to touch and be touched by majesty. Worship calls forth a fountain of deep feelings. Joy? Yes, and so much more; feeling-filled hearts that "throb and swell with joy" (Isaiah 60:5). Worship is a simple handshake and high drama, a kiss and a caressing, the mystery of earthquake and a still, small voice.

Worship is an adventure—the riding of wild horses, the push and pull, toss and tumble of a royal ballet. It is a high-wire act, March Madness, the wiping of blood off a knife. It is a sumptuous feast, poetry and priesthood, standing under a tree between flash and boom. It is the first kiss of lovers, the thrill of a countdown, the holding of live wires, the discovery of new planets and equations. It is a sudden rainbow, the milk and breast of a new mother, the tug on a child's fishing pole, a gingerly peek over a canyon wall, a quick rush across hot coals. It is a beckoning—an exhilarating walk through a minefield of love and wonder and power.

Such is worship and these are the kinds of feelings it should evoke. It should exhaust us, refresh us, inspire us, consume us and sometimes even terrify us. Though much more than our sentiments are involved, many real and very human feelings are released and realized in true worship. I'm not implying that we have to jump about like kangaroos, or clap like seals, or be noisy or even say anything at all—far from it! But worship must cost us emotionally and physically. Why? Because worship is about standing in front of God and all that God is. It is about me and *God*. It is about *me* and God.

2

Gift and Glory

In essence, there is only one thing God asks of us—
that we be people for whom God is everything and for
whom God is enough.

Brennan Manning

Who is greedier than a man for whom God is not
enough?

Augustine

True worship is a celebration and a deeply enriching experience. To paraphrase Clement of Rome, "Who is wiser than the man who sings and celebrates and holds a festival with God?" However, worship is also a serious endeavor, the encounter of mortal man with the immortal God.

How would you complete this sentence: "Worship is ..."? When was the last time you studied this subject in order to better glorify God and deepen your personal experience of worship? When did you last go to a worship service expecting to have a living encounter with the resurrected Christ? When did you last leave a worship service almost wordless, because you had touched—or rather, were touched by—the *mysterious tremendum*. Do you really hunger to be in the presence of God on the Lord's Day, and are you eager to encourage the congregation of saints?

How serious are you about the quality of your worship? Here is a test: When was the last time that you confessed to another Christian your lack of reverence or lack of effort and excellence in worship? Have you ever asked someone to hold you accountable for the sin of giving second best?

Worship really means something to God because he has deep feelings about us. And while God is certainly almighty, his heart can be wounded. In a sense, God has made himself vulnerable to us. His heart can be filled with pain, or he can rejoice over us with singing. We can please him, bringing him joy and honor; or we can grieve him by insult or flattery.

True worship is not always easy to achieve. Even sincere attempts to worship can become rote or ritual, mere habit or show, like the babbling prayers of the Pharisees. Or, we may fool ourselves into thinking that loud shouts and lots of amens are worship, as if outbursts of enthusiasm are equated to worship. They are not. Neither, by the way, is singing. These things are merely vehicles to express our worship. The key to worship lies in the heart behind these actions.

It was to the shame of the priests and people of Malachi's day that they did not realize they were doing wrong. If we are not careful, we may approach God on autopilot, sometimes focused, sometimes not. We may respond to God based on how we feel at the moment, rather than on the basis of his own worthiness. Worship is not a mood but a declaration. Our time with God can be costly, well planned and thoughtful, or casual, self-centered and meandering. As with any human relationship, God may feel special or he may feel slighted, cheated even.

However there is one important difference: Because he is our Creator and God, we are blessed, left empty-handed or even cursed as a result of our worship experience. Cain's offering was not just second-rate—it was an evil offering (1 John 3:12). Even under the new covenant of grace and truth, some Corinthians were put to death for not partaking of the Lord's Supper in a worthy manner (1 Corinthians 11:27-30). They did not *recognize* the seriousness of the situation. Again, imagine how heartbreaking it was for God to be in the midst of revealing to Moses the glory of tabernacle worship—the exact patterns, rich colors and intricate details—while at the foot of the same mountain, his newly-redeemed people were busy throwing earrings into a fire to make a cow. The contrast is startling: great, glorious and excellent versus lazy, sloppy and ungrateful.

What is God's opinion of my worship? Does he delight in it or despise it (Isaiah 1:9-17, Amos 5:22-23)? Does God invite it, or does he wish someone would shut the temple doors (Malachi 1:10)? In his temple, either we all cry "Glory," or we exchange our Glory for the image of a bull that eats grass (Psalm 106:20).

WORSHIP IS A PRIVILEGE

Worship is a gift and a privilege because salvation is a privilege. What a miracle that we are even breathing, let alone able to stand before God with his name on our lips. We were "without hope and without God in the world" (Ephesians 2:12), one breath, one heartbeat away from an eternity without God. But—by God's grace alone—we have been rescued and brought near to him. We are brought from graveyard to glory, from death to life, from stupidity to enlightenment, from nakedness and shame to the garments of kings and priests and sons of God.

It is a privilege to belong to God and to bear his name. It is a privilege to have access to his throne, with the ability to come freely before him, "confident and unashamed" (1 John 2:28). We have become God's treasured possession, his sons and daughters, a holy nation, a people belonging to God. Not only have we been forgiven, but we are assured of his forgiveness through the knowledge that God's own Spirit dwells within us. This is why worship is a privilege.

Under the old covenant, the Levites were especially gifted by God to be his priests. He was to be their portion and glory. In the new covenant, we are all priests of God (1 Peter 2:5, 9; Revelation 1:6). He has given us this blessing and great honor. In the Old Testament, the high priest was chosen by God. He did not assume this honor for himself, even as Christ was chosen by God to be our high priest. The high priest served as mediator between God and man. In the New Testament, Jesus Christ appears before God on our behalf, living to intercede for us.

> Therefore, brothers, since we have confidence *to enter the Most Holy Place* by the blood of Jesus, by a new and living

> way opened for us through the curtain, that is, his body, and since we have a great priest over the house of God, let us draw near to God with a sincere heart in *full assurance of faith*, having our hearts sprinkled to cleanse us from a guilty conscience and having our bodies washed with pure water. (Hebrews 10:19-22, emphasis mine)

Think of it, we have confidence to enter the Most Holy Place—not a copy, not a shadow, not on earth—but in heaven itself. This is the passage that startled me and compelled me to explore the subject of worship. A flaming arrow entered my heart, burning and soothing and burning again. It is impossible to understand, let alone communicate, the depth and privilege of this wonderful truth. It staggers the imagination. Here, perhaps more than anywhere else, we find ourselves in the center of miracles and signs and great wonders—in the very heart of God. Who would believe it if Scripture had not said so? That is why we should have "full assurance of faith."

The relationship of the old and new covenants has been described like this: The new within the old concealed, the old within the new revealed. Consider what an incredible privilege temple worship was; yet, we should not think God's desire for temple worship ended with the old covenant. There are a great many scriptures sprinkled throughout the New Testament to remind us that *we are the higher temple,* that the principles and privileges of worship in the old covenant are embedded and given greater glory in the New Testament. We don't have a physical altar; but we have a cross, we have a washing (Hebrews 10:22), we have a Passover lamb (1 Corinthians 5:7), we have bread and incense (John 6:35, Revelation 5:8), we have a spiritual circumcision (Romans 2:29), and we worship by the Spirit (Philippians 3:3). *We* are the temple, the dwelling of God (1 Corinthians 3:16). We offer sacrifices of praise (Hebrews 13:15), and our giving is like drink offerings to God (Philippians 2:17). We are clothed not with garments, but with the High Priest himself! (See Galatians 3:26-27.)

In the New Testament, everything is better, higher and holier. Our privileged position before God can hardly be described. We are covered with the blood of God's Son, not with the blood of goats. We serve in a temple not made with human hands, but built by God himself. Our high priest is high priest on the basis of an indestructible life, as one who lives forever to intercede for us. And we can come boldly and often into the Most Holy Place—something only the high priest could do but once a year and then, only briefly. We, on the other hand, may linger and gaze and rest. We do not merely approach the *Shekinah*, the glory of God; the *Shekinah* dwells within us! Our sacrifices are more holy than the bodies of sheep or goats: We are a royal priesthood, each of us is a temple, living stones, within the temple of God. If we are so privileged to serve God in this new and living way, surely worship must become our top priority.

WORSHIP IS PREEMINENT

The example and call to worship is plastered all over the Scriptures, from the first recorded offering by Cain and Abel to the final chorus of praise in the heavenly realms. The Scriptures take note of specific occasions when Abraham built altars, and not only Abraham, but his son, Isaac, and his grandson, Jacob, as well. The spark of the exodus was a call to worship—Moses pleaded on God's behalf, "Let my people go, so that they may worship me" (Exodus 7:16; 8:1, 20; 9:1, 13; 10:3). Worship encompassed the giving of the law, the tabernacle and the priesthood, the building of the temple, and the magnificent acts of adoration that accompanied it. It was for worship that musical instruments were built, the "Lord's musical instruments," and thousands of skilled men were trained to sing, play and write songs of praise to God—relevant, historical, urgent, God-inspired songs. The temple was a "twenty-four/seven" operation. The incense was to be kept burning, the bread of the Presence kept fresh, and the sacrifices were to be offered morning, noon and night.

The destruction of the temple, the place that bore God's sacred name, the epicenter of his glory and presence, signaled the ultimate downfall of the nation when they were exiled to Babylon. After the exile, the prophets who followed concerned themselves—almost exclusively—with the reconstruction of the temple, including the rebuilding of the wall of Jerusalem (Nehemiah), the restoration of the temple (Haggai), the renewal of the Law (Ezra) and the sacrifices that accompanied it (Malachi).

Throughout his word, God commands us to worship. He has always sought worshipers, and it is the great privilege of knowing God that calls forth our worship. Worship is taking place in the heavenly temple *right now*. And Jesus appears before God *today* on our behalf. The Holy Spirit lives in us at this very moment. As a church, we are being "built together to become a dwelling in which God lives by his Spirit" (Ephesians 2:22). We have come to thousands upon thousands of angels in joyful assembly, all worshiping God right now.

What does all this mean? We must become better and deeper worshipers, worshiping in spirit and in truth, with reverence and awe, full of praise and thanksgiving. In some of our assemblies we have no choice but to restore the glory of worship, to preach and teach and exemplify this subject, to worship better and more often, in private and public, with family and friends, in twos or ten thousands. When Israel left her God, the prophetic call was almost always a return to pure and proper worship. I believe for us as individuals, for the church, and for the sake of the world, we must restore and rededicate ourselves to the worship of God, perhaps more than anything else.

Just as Solomon wanted the temple to be great and awesome because God is great and awesome, our worship also must be the center of our life, our highest priority. As children of a new covenant, alive with God's Spirit, immersed in water and blood, we must appreciate the supreme privilege and the highest calling that compels us to worship God with all that we are.

WORSHIP IS OUR PURPOSE

To glorify God is our highest purpose and noblest work. This is our fundamental reason for being, and worship is an expression of this ultimate purpose. The best way to convey this is simply to let the Scriptures speak. In the next section, I will refer to one passage to make each point and give you others to study on your own. I encourage you to reflect on these words, allowing them to seep into your mind and heart, for they are the doorway to the heart and presence of God.

We are created for his glory.

> "Bring my sons from afar
>   and my daughters from the ends of the earth—
> everyone who is called by my name,
>   whom I created for my glory,
>   whom I formed and made." (Isaiah 43:6-7)

The next time you wonder or someone asks, "What's it all about?" remember the answer. Your life will either glorify God or disappoint him.

Also, study Isaiah 43:20-21, 60:21; Jeremiah 13:11 and Psalm 48:10-12.

We were called, chosen and redeemed for worship.

> But you are a chosen people, a royal priesthood, a holy nation, a people belonging to God, that you may declare the praises of him who called you out of darkness into his wonderful light. (1 Peter 2:9)

What did it cost God to pull you out of the darkness? Are you living up to your new "job description"—declaring his praises?

Also, look at Jeremiah 33:8-9 and Ephesians 3:20-21.

God's glory must be the rhyme and reason of all we do.

In Our Giving

> You will be made rich in every way so that you can be generous on every occasion, and through us your generosity will result in thanksgiving to God.
>
> This service that you perform is not only supplying the needs of God's people but is also overflowing in many expressions of thanks to God. Because of the service by which you have proved yourselves, men will praise God for the obedi-

> ence that accompanies your confession of the gospel of
> Christ, and for your generosity in sharing with them and with
> everyone else. (2 Corinthians 9:11-13)

It's too easy to let our financial giving become routine, as we regularly write checks that are part of our weekly budget. Take time to think about this passage. How many ways is God glorified when our giving is generous and free?

In Our Evangelism

> All this is for your benefit, so that the grace that is reaching
> more and more people may cause thanksgiving to overflow to
> the glory of God. (2 Corinthians 4:15)

Is God's grace reaching "more and more people" through you? Do you normally think of evangelism as a way to glorify God or to make you feel useful?

In Our Corporate Worship

> Then they worshiped him and returned to Jerusalem with
> great joy. And they stayed continually at the temple, praising
> God. (Luke 24:52-53)

Are your worship services truly worshipful, joyful, powerful? Where is your heart when the time comes to meet together and glorify God? See also Acts 4:23-30 and 1 Corinthians 14:24-25.

In Our Personal Example

> I eagerly expect and hope that I will in no way be ashamed, but
> will have sufficient courage so that now as always Christ will
> be exalted in my body, whether by life or by death.
> (Philippians 1:20)

How much is Christ exalted by your life—always? sometimes? seldom? Do you have sufficient courage (or whatever you need) to live in a way that honors him before others?

Also, look up Titus 2:3-10, 1 Corinthians 10:31 and Colossians 3:17.

In the Fellowship

> Every day they continued to meet together in the temple courts. They broke bread in their homes and ate together with glad and sincere hearts, praising God and enjoying the favor of all the people. And the Lord added to their number daily those who were being saved. (Acts 2:46-47)

Do your neighbors see "Acts 2" in your household? Are you giving, open and involved with your brothers and sisters in a way that draws others to God?

Also, look at Acts 4:32-35 and 5:12-16.

In Our Preaching and Teaching

> "We hear them declaring the wonders of God in our own tongues!" (Acts 2:11)

In my public communication, am I exalting God more than anything else? Am I lifting up his Son, making the teachings of God attractive? Am I speaking as though speaking the very "oracles of God" (1 Peter 4:11 KJV)?

Also look at Acts 5:42, 13:12 and Titus 2:7-10.

God's glory is the purpose of all created things.

> Praise the LORD, you his angels,
> > you mighty ones who do his bidding,
> > who obey his word.
> Praise the LORD, all his heavenly hosts,
> > you his servants who do his will.
> Praise the LORD, all his works
> > everywhere in his dominion.
>
> Praise the LORD, O my soul. (Psalm 103:20-22)

Stars, flowers, mountains, the elements, creatures, insects, every nation and power, visible and invisible—God has created them to gain glory for himself. God's eternal purpose, from beginning to end, is for the praise of his glorious grace (Ephesians 1:6, 12, 14). Never, ever will the whole assembly of heaven cease from declaring his glory (Revelation 4-5). Such awareness infuses each moment with wonder and praise. If even the stones and the trees glorify God, how much more should we! If all the angels shout for joy (Job 38:7), how much louder should we?

Also, read Psalm 148, 150:6 and John 15:7-8.

THE PROMISE OF WORSHIP

True worship is an expression of our true purpose and a declaration of God's worthiness. To worship God is to be in the very center of his will for our life. If we do what we are supposed to do and worship him acceptably, God blesses us and fills up our storehouses. He blesses our lands. He blesses our fields. He blesses our wombs. He blesses us richly—within and without. In fact, as we shall see, God takes special note of those who are jealous for his honor—rewarding, healing, saving, restoring, honoring and exalting them.

Worship is a supreme privilege. We must be sure that we convey this to our children and that they see us participating in and longing for the assembly of the saints. Even the journey to church should be an act of worship, a celebration of joy and anticipation. Our kids can read us— they often know exactly what we're feeling, like when we treat worship as a burden, or as just another weekly duty, or when we're tired, dragging our feet and disorganized. Worship is our privilege and purpose and must be experienced in a realm high above the mundane. God is worthy of the best, the most and the greatest that we can give, so let's show him this through joyful and excellent worship!

3

Mushroom, Star and Covenant Glory

*M*ushroom glory: One is grayish brown, small, found in most salad bars and is quite tasty; another, the luminous aftermath of a fifty-megaton nuclear bomb. If tasted, it would probably burn your lips.

Star glory: One is five pointed, drawn with crayon and hangs lovingly on your kitchen fridge; another kind, "the gleaming cantos of unvanquished space."[1] Just one of these, Eta Carinae is four million times brighter than our own star, the sun. It hangs upon, well, nothing!

Covenant glory: One is written on tablets of stone, delivered by angels on a mountain that could be seen and touched and involved the blood of bulls and goats and birds. Another is written on the tablets of human hearts, was brought to earth by God and cost the blood of our Creator, the Lord of heaven and earth, the Word of God himself (John 1:1). His blood not only forgives, but *glorifies* the sinner in his presence.

My next point cannot be overstated. The difference between the glory of the two mushrooms and the glory of the two stars, staggering as it is, is similar to the difference between the old and new covenants. The Old Testament was indeed glorious. Moses' face was radiant, the law was righteous, fading though it was. In fact, the law was "great and glorious" (Isaiah 42:21) and every decree righteous. The tabernacle and temple designs came from God's own mind, his own Spirit. And the blood of animals was a sacrifice of faith, and necessary.

---

[1] Michael Marten and John Chesterman, *The Radiant Universe* (Johannesburg: Clanose Publishers Ltd., 1980), 11.

But compared to the New Testament, Paul said that the old covenant was fading. In fact, the glory of the old has no glory *at all* compared to the glory of the new covenant (2 Corinthians 3:10). It has become, in the words of the Hebrew writer, "obsolete" (Hebrews 8:13). Christ himself crucified the law with its regulations and commandments (Colossians 2:14). And here my little analogy falls short. Why? Because as great as the differences are that separate the glories of mushrooms or stars, the degree of difference between the old and new covenants is immeasurably greater. One was temporary, "a copy and shadow, ...[a] pattern" (Hebrews 8:5); the other, true and living, the reality of heaven itself, eternal and glorious.

SENSE AND SENSIBILITY

Worship in the Old Testament, especially worship that centered around the tabernacle or temple, was a rich, complex, beautiful, mysterious and bloody affair. It involved all five of the senses: fragrances, colors and textures, trumpets and bells, meats and bitter herbs. Worshipers were enjoined to lift hands, kneel, bow, clap, stand, fall, dance and shout. Objects were measured, weighed, counted and marked off. Bodies were anointed, washed and shaven. Animals were handled and throats were cut. Blood was applied. The tabernacle was to be built by the most skilled and talented artists in Israel. In fact, God filled them with his Spirit to give them this ability. All the craftsmen were masters. Even those who mixed the anointing oils, "a fragrant blend" (Exodus 30:25), were skilled perfumers. The best and finest materials were used. Everything in the tabernacle, every last nail, was to be meticulously counted, exact, perfect. The reason? Because it was a pattern of the greater, more perfect tabernacle in heaven itself, "not built by human hands" (2 Corinthians 5:1), not "man-made" (Hebrews 9:24).

In the Old Testament, the high priest's clothing—the tunic, ephod, breastpiece, turban, sash and diadem—was consecrated with blood and oil. It could *never* be torn. He was not to perspire on it, so underneath he wore linen. No skin was to be showing. The diadem on his forehead was a sacred diadem, and he bore the words "holy to the Lord," or else his gifts would not be acceptable. Small bells, evenly spaced, were attached to the end of his tunic, and if sound could not be heard when he entered the temple, he would be put to death. The temple/tabernacle services were so sacred that if an Israelite was born from a foreign marriage, no one in that family could serve in the temple until ten generations had passed. Also, there were to be no physical deformities in the priests.

Every aspect of temple life was sacred to God. Blood was everywhere, on everything. Blood was shed even to purify mildew! The tabernacle *dust* was sacred. If a wife was suspected of adultery, the priest would take some dust from the tabernacle floor, mix it in a drink, and she would be forced to drink it to determine her guilt or innocence (see Numbers 5). The types of garments, down to the materials and colors, were chosen by God. Everything was "skillfully woven" (Leviticus 8:7). Whether dealing with furnishings and utensils, or the handling of the sacred vessels, everything about the tabernacle had to be done with the holiness of God in mind.

To safeguard his nation from pagan influence and to ensure that his worship and "set-apartness" were not tainted in any way, God wanted them to kill everything that breathed in the nations they would conquer. Israel was not to be corrupted by the world (Deuteronomy 20:16-18).

While Moses was on Mount Sinai, God gave him the Law, including the pattern and procedures of worship. They were inspired and utterly holy to the Lord. What other nation would have such awesome and holy laws (Deuteronomy 4:7-8)? What other people had such an awesome place to worship their God (1 Kings 8)?

A HOLY PRIESTHOOD

The priesthood was a gift and an honor bestowed by God on the tribe of Levi and on them alone. And from their number, only the sons of Aaron served in the temple. It may have been an exclusive group of men, but they also had the most dangerous job in the world. Everything had to be "exact," and "just like." They had to "make sure" and "be very careful." They were not to "linger," "not even for a moment." He commanded, "Don't touch"; "don't smell"; "don't look." God was not playing around! The design for the tabernacle and temple were from the Holy Spirit himself and had the purpose of showing us things that would take place in the future. The temple had to be respected.

As people of the twenty-first century, many times we are tempted to rush over the procedures in the book of Leviticus, not finding the ancient sacrificial system interesting or relatable. But as priests back then, we would have had to memorize those laws or we'd have been taking our life into our own hands. For the forty years in the wilderness that the Levites had to set up and take down the tabernacle furnishings, there was always a danger of doing something wrong, even by accident. Stringent measures needed to be taken to safeguard this (see Numbers 1:50-53; 3:10; 4:4-6, 15, 17-20). The priests served day and night. They kept the incense continually burning. They kept the bread of the Presence fresh. They guarded the sacred vessels—not to mention the fact that they sacrificed for the sins of the people. And they also held feasts and festivals. They killed, separated the organs and washed the blood from countless thousands of animals for their own sins and the sins of the people. And once a year, just once, on the Day of Atonement, the high priest was to enter the Most Holy Place. Even then, burning incense veiled the mercy seat from the naked gaze of their human eyes, and blood was applied. It was simple: Get in and get out.

AN OBEDIENT PEOPLE

Not only was the priesthood very specifically regulated, but so was the devotional life of the people. Everything was so specific. If you could not afford a lamb, then you were to give a pigeon or dove (see Jesus' birth in Luke 2:22-24). If not a bird, then a grain offering. And even with these, there were various laws determining how it was to be offered, based on whether it was grilled or baked or cooked. God was serious about his holiness and the honor of his name. He was to be respected, honored and set apart. The penalty for violating these sacred laws—death by stoning, stabbing, burning or burying alive—is woven throughout the Scriptures. In other words, "Don't come too close or you will die."

As mentioned earlier, if the bells on the high priest's robes were not heard when he entered the Most Holy Place, he would die (Exodus 28:35). Worshipers could gather for prayer and sacrifice in the temple courtyards, and there they could sing psalms as they saw their offerings presented to the Lord on his great altar. But if any person other than a Levitical priest (or other worship leader designated by God) attempted to enter the temple, he would die. If men and women made their own incense or anointing oils with the same proportions or ingredients as the sacred oils, to smell the beautiful fragrance, they would be cut off from the Israelites. If bodies were not washed, they would die. If God's name was blasphemed, they would die.

THE HOLINESS OF THE ARK

In the Holy of Holies, the heart of the temple, was the ark, which was a symbol of God's immediate presence among his people. The Bible calls the ark God's "splendor" and the "ark of his might" (Psalm 78:61). If human hands touched the ark, the penalty was death on the spot. In fact, the poles were always to be attached to the ark to safeguard against this. When the ark was carried, the Israelites were to stay *a thousand yards away.* If anyone looked at what was in the Most Holy Place besides the high priest, he would die. And if blood was not on the high priest himself when he entered the Most Holy Place, he would die.

Needless to say, when enemies of God got hold of the ark, they paid dearly for it. For example, when the Philistines captured the ark, God smashed their god Dagon, toppling him to the ground, and the Philistines were cursed by God with horrible boils. When they sent the ark back by oxen to placate the Jewish God, seventy men in a small town peeked inside, and guess what happened? They died (1 Samuel 6:19). In fact, *five hundred years* after the law was given that explained who should handle the ark and how, someone touched it, and guess what? He died.

The complexity and severity of old covenant worship was intended to provoke a sense of awe about who God was and the Israelites' relationship to him. It was designed to instill and promote care and caution. And it was a privilege of the highest order. What other nation had been taken whole, out of another nation? What other nation had such great laws? What other nation had a god who was near to them, who was their Presence? (See Deuteronomy 4:7-8.)

Why this elaborate setup? For several reasons. God's children must never, ever be lazy or sloppy in their worship of him. They were a sacred nation. No other nation had anything like the Israelites had. They were commanded to memorize all the commandments: learn, obey, recite, teach, memorize, learn, obey, recite, teach, memorize. Again and again, especially in Deuteronomy, God was showing that there was a great distinction between his people and himself, between himself and the gods of other nations. God was showing that he seeks worship, that we need to worship; that life is in the blood; that his people were his treasured possession; that worship was costly; that God himself was majestic in holiness and not to be trifled with; that everything associated with God is holy; and that all offerings to him became most holy offerings. It was indeed a covenant of glory, a covenant of great glory. But it was a covenant of death. It had no power to save anyone.

A WHOLE NEW WORLD

As we think about the Old Testament and the New Testament, the chasm cannot be wider. We worship in "the new way of the Spirit, and not in the old way of the written code" (Romans 7:6). Paul said, "The law is holy, and the commandment is holy, righteous and good" (Romans 7:12), and Isaiah said, "It pleased the LORD for the sake of his righteousness to make his law great and glorious" (Isaiah 42:21). But it was still a ministry that brought death. The fault, according to the writer of Hebrews, was not in the law, but in the people who could not keep the law. There was a necessity for a new covenant, a better covenant, a better way, "a new and living way" (Hebrews 10:20) through the Spirit and through the blood of Christ.

In the new covenant, everything has changed, become richer and deeper and more meaningful. Now we have Christ's blood. Now Christ is our high priest. He has entered the true tabernacle in the heavenly realms, not a man-made one. Now all may enter the Most Holy Place, through the curtain of Christ's own flesh, torn on our behalf (Hebrews 10:20). What a privilege! What a wonder! What a sacred responsibility!

A greater and more glorious covenant must evoke in us greater and more glorious worship. A better covenant should produce better worship. Divine blood should call forth deeper sacrifice. A living covenant should mean livelier singing. A covenant that brings grace and peace should make us hungry to be with God. Better, deeper, richer worship—not from laws and legalism, the blood of bulls and goats, but in spirit and in truth, "through the blood of the eternal covenant" (Hebrews 13:20). As the Hebrew writer put it,

> You have not come to a mountain that can be touched and that is burning with fire; to darkness, gloom and storm; to a trumpet blast or to such a voice speaking words that those who heard it begged that no further word be spoken to them, because they could not bear what was commanded: "If even an animal touches the mountain, it must be stoned." The sight was so terrifying that Moses said, "I am trembling with fear."
>
> But you have come to Mount Zion, to the heavenly Jerusalem, the city of the living God. You have come to thousands upon thousands of angels in joyful assembly, to the church of the firstborn, whose names are written in heaven. You have come to God, the judge of all men, to the spirits of righteous men made perfect, to Jesus the mediator of a new covenant, and to the sprinkled blood that speaks a better word than the blood of Abel.
>
> See to it that you do not refuse him who speaks. If they did not escape when they refused him who warned them on earth, how much less will we, if we turn away from him who warns us from heaven? At that time his voice shook the earth, but now he has promised, "Once more I will shake not only the earth but also the heavens." The words "once more" indicate the removing of what can be shaken—that is, created things—so that what cannot be shaken may remain.
>
> Therefore, since we are receiving a kingdom that cannot be shaken, let us be thankful, and so worship God acceptably with reverence and awe, for our "God is a consuming fire." (Hebrews 12:18-29)

THE GOD WE
WORSHIP

To be wholly obsessed with the glory of God is the consuming passion of the true worshiper, who lives to exalt God.

JOHN MACARTHUR, JR.

On the whole I do not find Christians, outside of the catacombs, sufficiently sensible, aware, of conditions. Does anyone have the foggiest idea what sort of power we so blindly evoke? Or, as I suspect, does no one believe a word of it? The churches are children, playing on the floor with their chemistry sets, mixing up a batch of TNT to kill a Sunday morning...it is madness to wear ladies' straw hats and velvet hats to church; we should all be wearing crash helmets. Ushers should issue life preservers and signal flares; they should lash us to our pews.

ANNIE DILLARD

Called from the world, we come together, deliberately seeking to approach reality at its deepest level by encountering God in and through Jesus Christ and by responding to this awareness.

JAMES WHITE

4

ENCOUNTER

HE WAS AFRAID AND SAID, "HOW AWESOME IS THIS
PLACE! THIS IS NONE OTHER THAN THE HOUSE OF GOD;
THIS IS THE GATE OF HEAVEN."

GENESIS 28:17

"WOE TO ME!" I CRIED. "I AM RUINED! FOR I AM A MAN
OF UNCLEAN LIPS, AND I LIVE AMONG A PEOPLE OF
UNCLEAN LIPS, AND MY EYES HAVE SEEN THE KING, THE
LORD ALMIGHTY."

ISAIAH 6:5

True worship springs from an encounter with God. We experience God in worship with the eyes of our heart. We taste and see that the Lord is good, and from this seeing, we respond. God surrounds his people "as the mountains surround Jerusalem" (Psalm 125:2). But like a mist that hides the mountain range, a veil covers our eyes from his glory. He is present, but hidden from our sight.

The Bible records several occasions when God pulled back this silky curtain for a brief moment and showed a hint of his glory and power to men. Each time he did, the encounter was overwhelming—if not outright terrifying. Whenever men have encountered God, no prompting was ever necessary. Instinctively, even unbelievers fell down to worship, overcome with awe. (See 1 Corinthians 14:25.)

In every such situation, men simply crumbled before God. When Belshazzar blasphemed God by using the temple vessels to toast his gods, a human hand appeared to write on the wall. At this, his face grew deathly pale, his knees started knocking together, and his legs gave way (Daniel 5:6). Isaiah was "undone," completely unraveled, when he saw the Holy One of Israel (Isaiah 6:5, KJV). After seeing visions of God, Ezekiel sat by the Kebar River, overwhelmed and appalled (Ezekiel 1:1, 3:15). Daniel fell prostrate, terrified and exhausted (Daniel 8:17, 27). Job covered his mouth and said, "I am reduced to dust and ashes" (Job 30:19). The soldiers at Jesus' tomb "shook and became like dead men" (Matthew 28:4) and the apostle John, after viewing the glorified Christ, "fell at his feet as though dead" (Revelation 1:17).

To see God face to face in the flesh is to die. Even Moses, who had requested to see the glory of God, was told,

> "...you cannot see my face, for no one may see me and live."
> Then the LORD said, "There is a place near me where you may stand on a rock. When my glory passes by, I will put you in a cleft in the rock and cover you with my hand until I have passed by. Then I will remove my hand and you will see my back; but my face must not be seen." (Exodus 33:20-23)

In poetic language, "the mountains melt like wax before the LORD" (Psalm 97:5). The heavens and the earth flee from his presence, because "there [is] no place for them" (Revelation 20:11). When the day of judgment comes, evil itself will be vanquished at the sight of God's splendor (2 Thessalonians 2:8). Men will cry out for mountains to fall on them to hide them from "the wrath of the Lamb" (Revelation 6:16). But there will be no mountains to fall on them; they will all have melted or fled.

ENTER HIS COURTS

Of course, God's revelation of himself is not always so dramatic. However, he is the same God Almighty today, unchanged and immutable—"majestic in holiness, awesome in glory, working wonders" (Exodus 15:11). He is just as real, just as near.

Although God is everywhere at once and fills our universe, worshiping him brings about a special encounter with his presence—in a particular time and place. We should remember that Israel was "to appear" before the Lord, "to assemble as one man" in his presence, "to gather before him" at the tent of meeting, "to eat in his presence" at the festivals and feasts, and "to enter his courts with praise." When we collectively worship God today, we consecrate a specific occasion in space and time to gather before the Eternal, ever-present One.

Jesus taught that "where two or three come together in my name, there am I with them" (Matthew 18:20). He is always with us, but this declaration refers to his presence in a special sense. Paul referred to this when he wrote to the Corinthians: "When you are assembled in the name of our Lord Jesus and I am with you in spirit, and *the power of our Lord Jesus is present*" (1 Corinthians 5:4, emphasis mine). In context, both of these verses refer to Jesus being present for specific acts of judgment and church discipline; they illustrate, however, that he is "there" in a special sense when we come together as a body. Later on, concerning the Lord's Supper, Paul wrote, "Anyone who eats and drinks without *recognizing* the body of the Lord eats and drinks judgment on himself" (1 Corinthians 11:29, emphasis mine). We must remember each and every Sunday that it is the Lord's Day, the Lord's Supper, and that the Lord is in our midst, powerfully and markedly present. He walks among the lampstands, the churches, with blazing eyes that penetrate our fellowship, searching out hearts and minds, blessing the sons of Barnabas and cursing the sons of Ananias (Acts 4-5; Revelation 2-3).

Worship proceeds from this kind of encounter, this *heightened awareness* of God's presence. God reveals himself to us and we respond to that revelation. We may respond to his love, the cross, his creation, his sovereignty, or his works on our behalf. He is the I AM, the audience of one. "I am the LORD, your Holy One, Israel's Creator, your King" (Isaiah 43:15).

The more aware we are that God is in our midst, the truer and richer our worship experience will be. If we are not conscious of God when we pray or sing or have communion, we are not worshiping at all, but we are praying to ourselves like a Pharisee or simply "speaking into the air" (1 Corinthians 14:9). If we do not grasp that God is there, we are not bowing in worship; we are just babbling on. If we fail to comprehend just who is calling us to sacrifice, we are not giving financially to God, but to a plate. Imagine a couple on a date, sitting at a table and having a conversation. Wouldn't it seem odd if they never looked at one another, never made eye contact, but simply let their eyes wander as they "talked"? Our worship can easily degenerate to this point if we are not focused on the reality of God's presence—not just within us, but in our midst.

I will never forget a conversation I had with Martin Bentley almost eighteen years ago. He said to me, like it was the eleventh commandment or as if he were Moses himself, "Henry, don't bore your angels." What a thought! Truly, we have come to "thousands upon thousands of angels in joyful assembly" (Hebrews 12:22), joyful because they stand in the presence of God (Matthew 18:10). We must surely bore our angels when we live uncourageous lives; but worse, we must embarrass them whenever we worship in meager, paltry, halfhearted ways. Why? Because we are privileged to have a relationship with God that the angels can only long for. We are the bride of Christ, the wife of the Lamb, the reason for the universe; angels are his servants. They see things we don't, but we have what angels long for (1 Peter 1:12). Should the attendants to the groom be more fired up than the bride herself? Hardly. However, this can happen when we content ourselves with just coming to church rather than encountering the Presence.

Worship is the divine/human moment, where God, to borrow a phrase from R. C. Sproul, "invades the human soul."[1] This is why David's worship of God was so rich. Read the Psalms and take note of how immediate God was to David. David was fully engaged—recalling, reciting, reminding, recounting, rejoicing—because he "saw" his God so completely in every part of his life. This is the kind of worship that we must strive to emulate, to embrace with our whole being. God is here for us and his invitation is sure: "Open wide your mouth and I will fill it"

---

[1] R. C. Sproul, *In the Presence of God* (Nashville: Word Publishing, 1999), 86.

(Psalm 81:10); "be still and know" (Psalm 46:10); "take off your sandals" (Exodus 3:5); "kneel before the Father" (Ephesians 3:14); "prepare to meet your God" (Amos 4:12); "enter his gates with thanksgiving and his courts with praise" (Psalm 100:4); "consecrate yourselves" (Joshua 3:5).

When we allow God this far into our hearts, we pray by the Spirit, worship by the Spirit and sing spiritual songs with spiritual words. Then God is most glorified in us because we are most satisfied with him. We are enveloped, filled and confronted by his Presence. We have come into his wonderful light, and here we fully declare his praise. This is our summoning to the throne of grace. Here we taste his mystery and are touched by his majesty.

In this house of God, this Bethel, we behold his power and glory and feast on his love. Here we are found by him who seeks our worship. Here we are awakened by the living One, carried off by the Beloved, aware of our Creator, embraced and lifted and kissed by our *Abba*, our Father. And here we are sheltered in his presence and surrounded with songs of deliverance (Psalm 32:7). Here, in this sacred hiding place, we are safest, and our hearts find strength and rest. Not only is this peace, this rest, an expression of worship, but it must also bring immense pleasure to God. Worship springs and flows first and foremost from our encounter with God.

Deeper Awareness

If you are anything like me, you forget, from time to time, that you are in the presence of Almighty God when you worship. In fact, you probably forget this lots of times. To my shame, I cannot count how many times I have come to a church service, sung about Jesus, partaken of the Lord's Supper, enjoyed Christian fellowship, given to the poor, read and prayed in Jesus' name, but was—amazingly—unaware of God's presence. Not that I was thinking about sports or shoes or the color of the curtains (although I've done that too); but deep within, on a fundamental level, I was wandering, unfocused or simply running on autopilot. This is a form of irreverence, even unbelief, which is really no worship at all.

Sadly, even our most worshipful moments may be corrupted. But this should not surprise us. We are frail, and because worship is so important, we should expect that Satan would attack us and try to distract us. During what should be the most intimate time of worship, participating in the Lord's Supper, it is possible to have silly thoughts, extremely sinful and wicked thoughts. Hopefully this is not common, but it does happen. Remember the first Lord's Supper? As soon as Judas took the bread from Jesus, Satan entered into him (John 13:27). Therefore, we must not be discouraged. God knows we are frail and forgetful, little pieces of distraction and dust. We should not beat ourselves up when this happens; rather, we need to gently recall and remind ourselves what we are a part of—often, if necessary. Then we must confess in silence and continue in worship. We should not flog ourselves. "It is for freedom that Christ has set us free" (Galatians 5:1).

APPREHENDING GOD

How can we more clearly apprehend this invisible God during public worship? I believe a crucial key is what we do during the other six days. We must apprehend God in the details of each day, not just on Sunday. This was the intent, even the glory, of Israel's law.

Like the psalmist, we must pray, "Open my eyes that I may see wonderful things in your law" (Psalm 119:18). Leviticus is not dry reading; it embodies the majesty of God's holiness, his set-apartness. It contains "wonderful things." Similarly, the temple rituals are not sleeping pills; they are a treasure house of riches if we just open our eyes. The law forced Israel, by hook or by crook, into an awareness of God. Its legislation touched every aspect of Jewish life—planting, harvesting, cleaning and cooking, clothing and beards, cups and kettles, seeds and lands, animals and offerings, sickness and sacrifices, lending and borrowing, menstruation and marriage, mildew and molds, even the burying of human excrement—because "the LORD your God moves about in your camp" (Deuteronomy 23:14). They were commanded to love God and his word twenty-four/seven. God's word was to be read to them, bound to them, tied to them; placed on their doors, their tassels, their gates; and to be spoken of, discussed and memorized from morning till evening. God did this so Israel would have to think of him—more than that, to include him.

There is a lesson here. If we do not include God in the small stuff, in the "ordinary," how can we apprehend God in the greater things—like worship? Said Paul,

> Whether you eat or drink or *whatever you do,* do it all for the glory of God. (1 Corinthians 10:31, emphasis mine)

> Give thanks in *all circumstances.* (1 Thessalonians 5:18, emphasis mine)

> The Lord is near. Do not be anxious about *anything.* (Philippians 4:5-6, emphasis mine)

> *Set your minds* on things above, not on earthly things. (Colossians 3:2, emphasis mine)

> Take captive *every thought* to make it obedient to Christ. (2 Corinthians 10:5, emphasis mine)

Like Paul, David also lived by this truth.

> I have set the LORD *always* before me. (Psalm 16:8, emphasis mine)

God was so real, so immediate to David. David was not just aware, but intensely aware of God.[2] We cannot see God, in the words of William Blake, with this "mortal and perishing eye," but we don't have to. God is obvious to all who walk by faith and not by sight. As Asaph observed,

> Your path led through the sea,
>   your way through the mighty waters,
>   though your footprints were not seen. (Psalm 77:19)

---

[2] Psalm 18 is one example. Did God rescue David from Saul in the nick of time by sending a storm? Is this David's poetic expression of this?

RENDEZVOUS

In order to deepen our awareness of God's presence during our times of worship, carefully consider the following suggestions.

Open your eyes. "My Father is always at his work," said Jesus (John 5:17). God is working on our behalf. From the miraculous to the mundane, God is orchestrating the details of our lives—the timing of intersections, the exchange of words, the disposition of others toward us, good things and bad things, sleepless nights and stray arrows—even in suffering, especially in suffering (Romans 8:28).

Consider Joseph—the hatred of his brothers, the coat, the dreams, the well, the sentiments of Reuben, the Midianite caravan, Potiphar's house, his good looks, the lust of a woman, accusations of rape, imprisonment, dreams and interpretations, forgotten favors and so much more. And then, after thirteen years of setbacks and humiliation, Joseph went from pit to pinnacle in one day. Joseph became "second-in-command" and "father to Pharaoh" for "the saving of many lives" (Genesis 41:43, 45:8, 50:20). Where was God during all that time? "The LORD was with Joseph" (Genesis 39:2, 23).

God is the great conductor, leading our lives in the harmony of his purpose with a symphony of circumstance. If we are inattentive or insensitive to God's presence during the rest of the week, how can there be any real awareness of God in our moments of worship?

Believe.

> Now faith is being sure of what we hope for and certain of what we do not see. This is what the ancients were commended for. (Hebrews 11:1-2)

> And without faith it is impossible to please God, because anyone who comes to him must believe that he exists and that he rewards those who earnestly seek him. (Hebrews 11:6)

> By faith he left Egypt, not fearing the king's anger; he persevered because he saw him who is invisible. (Hebrews 11:27)

> Let us draw near to God with a sincere heart in full assurance of faith. (Hebrews 10:22)

Like belief, unbelief is also powerful. So powerful, in fact, that it can blind us from "the light of the knowledge of the glory of God in the face of Christ" (2 Corinthians 4:6). This was the difference between Elisha and his servant Gehazi. Gehazi could not see and was afraid, whereas Elisha could see and was at peace. "O Lᴏʀᴅ, open his eyes," he prayed. "Then the Lᴏʀᴅ opened the servant's eyes, and he looked and saw the hills full of horses and chariots of fire all around Elisha" (2 Kings 6:17). Elisha did not summon the angels; they were already present. He knew it, but Gehazi did not.

Ask. "You do not have, because you do not ask God" (James 4:2). Elisha asked. So did Paul: "I pray also that the eyes of your heart may be enlightened" (Ephesians 1:18). Moses did: "Show me your glory" (Exodus 33:18), and so did David: "One thing I ask" (Psalm 27:4).

Desire. God wants to show himself to us, but he is subtle. He is a declarer who hides himself, not only in hard times, during the "dark night of the soul,"[3] but as an ongoing test of our hunger for him. He blesses the searcher and the seeker (Proverbs 2:1-5). He invites us, asking, "Who is he who will devote himself to be close to me?" (Jeremiah 30:21). He rewards those who come to him and earnestly seek him (Hebrews 11:6). "Delight yourself in the Lᴏʀᴅ and he will give you the desires of your heart" (Psalm 37:4). Again we take our cues from David, perhaps the preeminent worshiper in all of Scripture.

> One thing I ask of the Lᴏʀᴅ,
>   this is what I seek:
> that I may dwell in the house of the Lᴏʀᴅ
>   all the days of my life,
> to gaze upon the beauty of the Lᴏʀᴅ
>   and to seek him in his temple. (Psalm 27:4)

> As the deer pants for streams of water,
>   so my soul pants for you, O God.
> My soul thirsts for God, for the living God.
>   When can I go and meet with God? (Psalm 42:1-2)

---

[3] A book of spiritual poetry by this name was written by the sixteenth century Spanish mystic St. John of the Cross.

Again, David's desire for God is clearly seen in the following Psalm:

> O God, you are my God,
>   earnestly I seek you;
> my soul thirsts for you,
>   my body longs for you,
> in a dry and weary land
>   where there is no water.
>
> I have seen you in the sanctuary
>   and beheld your power and your glory.
> Because your love is better than life,
>   my lips will glorify you.
> I will praise you as long as I live,
>   and in your name I will lift up my hands.
> My soul will be satisfied as with the richest of foods;
>   with singing lips my mouth will praise you.
> On my bed I remember you;
>   I think of you through the watches of the night.
> (Psalm 63:1-6)

Notice, he deeply desires; he knows what he wants; he states his affection; he makes a promise; and he is certain of the blessing. God is David's magnificent obsession, his hunger, his longing, his life. He cannot stop himself—even on his bed in the middle of the night, he just wants God.

Consecrate and pray. The act of setting our hearts for worship—washing ourselves by confession, anticipating our encounter with God—prepares a way for the Lord. It is a "Yes" to the invitation and an "Amen" to the promise of reward.

Recall. Remind. Remember. "Be still, and know" (Psalm 46:10)—quiet yourself and just be aware of God. God knows we are weak, and he is gracious. We may have to gently remind ourselves of this several times during the service, but that's okay. At the same time, if we are distracted too much, we have a problem that needs to be confessed and talked about.

Bring your burdens. Why do disciples pray to leave their anxious burdens outside? This is distracting. Instead, bring them in, according to the apostle Peter, and cast them on God, who gives us peace (1 Peter 5:7). Then hopefully, the peace of God will guard our hearts and minds in Christ Jesus.

Participate fully. Train yourself to be engaged in the whole service. Open your Bible, sing out and follow the prayers—word for word, if necessary. Then your "Amens" will really mean something. It may be difficult at times, but we must not allow others to affect the quality of our own worship before God. David had to deal with women like Michal. Hannah had to deal with men like Eli's sons. Daniel had his satraps and lions. Anna had the Sadducees. But it was always, only, Anna and her King, not Anna and her Caiphas. Was Jesus hindered because the synagogue was full of Pharisees? Were Paul and Silas hindered because they were in prison, naked, beaten and surrounded by hostile men? Not at all. In fact, without a shred of self-consciousness or complaining, they "were praying and singing hymns to God" (Acts 16:25).

Those who lead us in worship must really lead. It is a great privilege and a great responsibility to bring us into the presence of God, so to speak. However, even if those who are leading are "not helping any" because of a lack of skill or maturity—why should that rob me of a great worship experience? If Christ is in our midst, great worship is always possible.

Our worship leaders, like all who lead us, are servants of God and gifts to the church (Ephesians 4:10-11). Some are stronger than others, more dynamic, more experienced, and yes—better singers! Nevertheless Christ is in the least of them.

Let us sing to Christ himself, as if Christ is beside us, as if Christ is our songleader, as if Christ himself is the giver of bread and wine. Taking this to heart, every time of worship will be an encounter with our God.

5

CORAM DEO

Suddenly the mole felt a great awe that turned his muscles to water, bowed his head and rooted his feet to the ground. It was no panic terror—indeed he felt wonderfully at peace and happy—but it was an awe that smote him and, without seeing, he knew could only mean some August Presence was very, very near.

HEINZ SEELIG

To worship is to come into the presence of God. Every would-be worshiper must know with certainty that God exists and rewards those who earnestly seek him (Hebrews 11:6). Every blood-covered child of God stands before him in the Most Holy Place in heaven itself and must draw near in sincerity and full assurance of faith (Hebrews 10:19-22).

IN HIS PRESENCE

What does it mean to stand *Coram Deo,* "in the very presence of God"? Being in the presence of God is to be *surrounded by splendor.* God is magnificent in splendor, a vast and terrifying splendor. We approach him who dwells in unapproachable light, resplendent with light. (See 1 Timothy 6:16 and Psalm 76:4.)

In his presence we *encounter the Holy One.* God is majestic in holiness—utterly, radically and altogether unlike anything in all creation. He is wholly other, altogether unlike us. He is transcendent, set apart, high above, utterly beyond. God is so holy that his angels, sinless beings themselves, are overwhelmed by their Creator's holiness, crying out day and night, "Holy, holy, holy" (Isaiah 6:3, Revelation 4:8). He is a consuming fire and a jealous God; a God who despises, abhors, detests and banishes sin from his presence.

In his presence we are *embraced and entangled by love.* "God is love" (1 John 4:8). He is our lover and we are his beloved. God's grace and love have been lavished upon us (Ephesians 1:4-7). We are challenged and encouraged, "together with all the saints, to grasp how wide and long and high and deep" is this love—"and to know this love that surpasses knowledge—that you may be filled to the measure of all the fullness of God" (Ephesians 3:18-19).

In God's presence we are *confronted by reality.* Reality 101. By faith, Moses "saw him who is invisible" (Hebrews 11:27), and by faith we too see him who is invisible. God is veiled, silent to our ears and hidden from our senses; but he is here now, in the fullness of his being. He is more real than all the radio and television waves that are currently bouncing off our walls. We are blissfully unaware of the presence of this seething ocean of energy until we turn on a television or a radio, but they are there—and so is God. He is not bouncing around anywhere; but is always I AM (Exodus 3:14). He is the God who sees me and takes note. He is closer than my hands, nearer than a kiss, more vital, more immanent than the air I breathe. He is as all-pervading as the oxygen that fills my lungs and passes into my bloodstream, ultimately nourishing every cell in my body.

In his presence we are *enveloped by glory and greatness.* "Great is the LORD and most worthy of praise; his greatness no one can fathom" (Psalm 145:3). "Who can proclaim the mighty acts of the LORD or fully declare his praise?" (Psalm 106:2). God's greatness crushes human imagination, flattens the wisdom and sophistry of men, blasts and lays low every trace of arrogance or pride. In fact, this is God's own proof of his deity (see Job 40:9-14). Everything God has made declares his glory and greatness—every star, a herald; every flower, a cathedral; every element, an oracle; every man and woman, an image-bearer. They all declare his divine nature and eternal power, the vastness of his wisdom and the beauty of his being. It is before this God that we speak and pray.

In his presence we are *engaged with unspeakable power*. He is *El Shaddai*, "God Almighty" (Genesis 17:1). His power, his eternal power, ignites every flaming orb and sustains every living thing. He has only to breathe—only to *will*—to create. He "speaks and summons the earth" (Psalm 50:1) and knows every star by name and "calls things that are not as though they were" (Romans 4:17). *Ex nihilo*, "out of nothing," he made the universe and all that is in it. He opens his hand and satisfies the desires of every living thing (Psalm 145:16).

We do not simply come to church, we are *summoned by a king*. We do not summon God, he summons us. God is the King of all kings and the Lord of lords. "I am a great king," says the LORD Almighty, "and my name is to be feared among the nations" (Malachi 1:14). "He does as he pleases with the powers of heaven and the peoples of the earth" (Daniel 4:35). All nations are as nothing before him, a drop of water in his hand, a particle of dust on his robe. None can say to him, "What have you done?" or "Why are you doing it?" No one can thwart his plans or his purposes. He is the King of glory. Every authority and every power is created and exists for him. Visible and invisible, they were created by him, for him. He is the ruler of all things, and he rules with invincible conviction. He treats every pagan king as his "servant" (Jeremiah 25:9), his "chosen ally" (Isaiah 48:14), his "ax" (Isaiah 10:15), his "washbasin" (Psalm 60:8), his "anointed" (Isaiah 45:1) and his "shepherd" (Isaiah 44:28) to fulfill his purposes. What they conspire, God decrees (Acts 4:27-28). They cast off, but God coronates (Psalm 2). They do, but God determines. As seen in the Scriptures, every king, every official, every government agent is God's servant to restore Israel, to rebuild the temple, to discipline other nations, to serve the church and the eternal purposes of God (Ephesians 1:21-23); and when they have finished serving him, they become the food of maggots (Isaiah 14:11). When kings disagreed with God on this point, God turned them into cows, their rivers into blood and their civilizations into piles of sand. He is the King of kings.

In his presence I *taste and immerse* myself in the blood of my Redeemer.

> Oh, precious is the flow,
> That makes me white as snow;
> No other fount I know,
> Nothing but the blood of Jesus.[1]

We belong to Jesus. He owns us. His blood, the eternal blood of the eternal covenant, has purchased us (Acts 20:28). We are no longer our own. Plunged into the blood of Immanuel's veins, we have "redemption through his blood, the forgiveness of sins" (Ephesians 1:7). "Without the shedding of blood there is no forgiveness" (Hebrews 9:22). We eat his flesh and drink his blood (John 6:53); blood poured, blood shed, blood sprinkled, blood washed; blood that purifies, cleanses, whitens, sanctifies; divine blood, precious blood, blood that raises the dead. Christ is the blood on my clothing, my heart and my conscience. He is the blood in my mouth and the blood on my doorframe, a Lamb that was slaughtered before the creation of the world (Revelation 13:8). Can we be blind to so much blood or indifferent to such a great and costly salvation? Shall we treat as an unholy thing the blood of the covenant that sanctifies us (Hebrews 10:29) or participate "in an unworthy manner" (1 Corinthians 11:27) in the body and blood of Christ at the Lord's Supper? What if God were to open our eyes to see such vast amounts of blood—divine blood, the blood of our Creator? To drink in an unworthy manner is to destroy our own souls. To understand this blood and its beauty and its power is to praise God with our whole being. The centerpiece of heaven is a Lamb that was slain (Revelation 5).

It is this God whom we worship, this God whom we encounter, and into the presence of this God—who is with us, who hears us, who takes note, who blesses and curses our worship—that we come. Let us be still and know. Let us take off our shoes, bow low, give thanks and worship acceptably, with reverence and awe.

---

[1] Lyrics by Robert Lowry, "What Can Wash Away My Sin?" *Songs of the Kingdom,* 2nd ed. (Woburn, Mass.: Discipleship Publications International, 1999), song 380.

GOD NOTICES

The Righteous One takes note. (Proverbs 21:12)

From heaven the LORD looks down
    and sees all mankind;
from his dwelling place he watches
    all who live on earth—
he who forms the hearts of all,
    who considers everything they do. (Psalm 33:13-15)

[Hagar] gave this name to the LORD who spoke to her: "You are the God who sees me," for she said, "I have now seen the One who sees me." (Genesis 16:13)

Obviously when we worship, we have God's full attention. But the question really should be, does God have my full attention? It makes no difference if I am in a congregation of thousands, of two or three, or alone in my closet. Whether in public or in private, all worship is personal. God knows what is in our hearts and minds when we sing or worship or pray. Every motive is weighed. Every secret is accounted for. Every desire acknowledged, whether we are bored or blissful, happy or hurting. And based on me, as an individual in his presence, he accepts my worship or he does not. I may be in a row with ten other Christians, but God sees *me*. What am *I* offering to God?

The Scriptures take pains to let us know that God notices the individual in a crowd and takes note of his or her heart.

Then those who feared the LORD talked with each other, and the Lord listened and heard. A scroll of remembrance was written in his presence concerning those who feared the LORD and honored his name.

"They will be mine," says the LORD Almighty, "in the day when I make up my treasured possession. I will spare them, just as in compassion a man spares his son who serves him. And you will again see the *distinction* between the righteous and the wicked, between those who serve God and those who do not." (Malachi 3:16-18, emphasis mine)

Here are several examples of God singling out, distinguishing, separating, noticing and making a distinction.

- Abel's offering was better than Cain's. Both gave, both sacrificed. But "the Lord looked with favor on Abel and his offering, but on Cain and his offering he did not look with favor" (Genesis 4:4-5). He does not separate a man from his offering. They are one and the same. If you give something halfheartedly, that is who you are.

- It was only after the debacle of Saul's sins that he built an altar to the Lord (1 Samuel 14:35).

- Many people pressed around Jesus, but only one really touched him, causing power to go out from him (Mark 5:24-30).

- Solomon made gold shields, but his son replaced them with bronze (2 Chronicles 12:9-10).

- Jesus noticed the poor widow who "put in more than all the others" (Luke 21:3).

- The exiles all repaired their sections of the wall, except for one man, Baruch, who "zealously repaired" his section (Nehemiah 3:20). You may do better than I, but I counted thirty-eight examples of repairing sections of the wall. Only one was zealously repaired, and it was noted.

- Ananias and Sapphira lied to God, not to men (Acts 5:1-4).

- God notices one man, from one family, from one tribe, from one nation—Achan—who desecrated the name of his God (Joshua 7:19-23).

- Concerning the woman who had poured perfume on his feet, Jesus said, "She has done a beautiful thing to me" (Mark 14:6). Only Christ understood the significance of this gesture.

- "A few people in Sardis who have not soiled their clothes" (Revelation 3:4) were commended by Jesus.

- "Do not be afraid, Zechariah; your prayer has been heard" (Luke 1:13).

- Each altar Abraham built is noted and recorded (Genesis 12:7-8, 13:18, 22:9).

- "The Bereans were of more noble character than the Thessalonians" (Acts 17:11).

- Although Jehu was a great destroyer of Baal worship, he "was not careful to keep the law...with all his heart" (2 Kings 10:31).

- In the book of Nehemiah, those who volunteered to live in Jerusalem were all counted and named (Nehemiah 11:1-24).

- When the tabernacle was first dedicated, every offering by all twelve tribes was counted, measured and reported, although all twelve offerings were all exactly the same (Numbers 7). What appears monotonous to us is important to God. A message is being sent—God cares about the details.

I recently surveyed a number of disciples regarding their understanding of what takes place in worship. Surprisingly, very few—including songleaders—thought of worship as an encounter with God's presence. We live out our lives in a 3-D world where it is only possible to be in one place at any given time. It is easy to forget that God is everywhere. And it demands faith to know that he is not just present, but keenly aware and attentive. He notices. He feels. He waits. And he longs to hide us in the shelter of his presence (Psalm 31:20). What a privilege! What an opportunity! Let us run to the encounter with our gracious and fearsome God.

> You have made known to me the path of life;
> you will fill me with joy in your presence,
> with eternal pleasures at your right hand. (Psalm 16:11)

6

OCEAN OF MERCY

Was it from a couch
Or from heaven he arose that night?
Was it to the floor
Or to the earth he descended that night?
Was it with towel
Or human flesh he wrapped himself that night?
Was it with water
Or with blood he washed them clean that night?
Was it to his table
Or to his throne he ascended that night?
That night!
That night!
That staggering night!
When men argued for greatness
And God was on his knees.

H. K.

The best verse in the Bible, to me, is also one of the shortest: "God is love" (1 John 4:16). Not only does God do loving things, but the core of his being, that which pervades all that he is and prompts all that he does, is love. God is love. This means that love is at the heart of the universe. Love—divine love—is the reason we are here. It is the reason we are called to heaven. It is the reason Jesus died for us. God's love is perfect and boundless. What are the height and depth and width of

God's love? His love is unsearchable, immeasurable, inexpressible, infinite in all directions, but fully focused on each of us. God is attentive to the fall of the sparrow, and "you are worth more than many sparrows," said Jesus (Luke 12:7).

DAYA SAGAR

When we lived in India, two things were said about Jesus that I treasure to this day. The first was a local title given to him in a theatrical production about his life: Daya Sagar or "Ocean of Mercy." What a rich summary of his life! Deep and inviting, love without limits, an ocean without shores. The other statement came from a villager in the south of India. His name was Venkatesh Raman. Sadly and remarkably, he had not heard one word about Christ during his entire life. He only saw a picture of him on the cross one day when he ventured outside of his village. When I first met him in Mumbai (Bombay), he said to me, "Tell me about the god who died." It was wonderful!

India has countless thousands of gods, goddesses and local deities. For instance, in Bombay they worship Ganesh, a roly-poly god of prosperity; in Calcutta, they revere Kali, the dark side of god; and the names of the Hindu pantheon go on and on. I have seen more than a million Indians carry effigies of Ganesh throughout the city of Bombay to Juhu beach, where they cast them into the sea. The whole spectacle was surreal: thousands of idols of all sizes, made with varying degrees of skill and expense, carried by individuals, families or entire neighborhoods, now floating in the ocean. The next morning when the tide had gone out, the scene was eerie. Before my eyes stretched a landscape of broken pieces of painted clay, tinfoil and jewelry in the shape of limbs, elephant heads and bellies of boys' bodies, all of which either stuck in the sand or floated, bobbing up and down in the water for miles out into the Arabian Sea. Sincere or not, all these acts of worship, meant to placate Ganesh or Kali or a myriad of other such gods, are horrid in their distortion of the true God's nature and being. This is why idolatry is so offensive, so shocking to God.

When Mr. Raman asked about "the god who died," I felt like Paul at the Acropolis, preaching about the "unknown god" (Acts 17:23). Of all the things Mr. Raman could have known about Jesus, he only knew one thing, which happens to be the best thing of all: Christians worship the God who died. Who else can say that? Who can imagine it? The Creator dies for his creation. To the pagan world, it is fantasy; to the Jews, appalling; to a Muslim, a lie because God would never let that happen to his Son. But to us who know and believe and love him, we can say with Peter, "You killed the author of life" (Acts 3:15), and with Paul, "[You] crucified the Lord of glory" (1 Corinthians 2:8). There is no better way to express God's love than Jesus on the cross.

The Enfleshment of Love

Jesus is the perfect expression of God's love. If God had a body of blood and bone, eyes, ears and hands like me, what would he be like? What would the invisible, eternal God of love look like in action, fully engaged with men and women—who are steeped in sin, ignorance and unbelief? How would he enter this world? How would he live? How would he die? This is who Jesus Christ is: God in human flesh, *the ocean of mercy in a single drop of water*. He is eternal but contained, holy but touchable, boundless but in a body. Jesus is the incarnation, the enfleshment, of the verse "God is love."

In the Old Testament, God is portrayed again and again as a God of love and of intense feeling. He is our Father, our Shepherd, our Husband, our Redeemer, our Savior and our friend. God is pictured as bending down to feed us, as carrying us "close to his heart" and "on his shoulders" (Isaiah 40:11; Luke 15:5). He *enjoyed* his people. Finding Israel was "like finding grapes in the desert" (Hosea 9:10). He remembered with longing the affection of his beloved. "I remember the devotion of your youth," he said, "how as a bride you loved me and followed me through the desert" (Jeremiah 2:2). Even when God had to judge them, he would never abandon them completely. "How can I...?" he agonizes, "My heart is changed within me; all my compassion is aroused" (Hosea 11:8). God was and is deeply jealous for us. We are "the apple of his eye" (Deuteronomy 32:10), "engraved...on the palms of [his] hands" (Isaiah 49:16). Even if a nursing woman would "forget the baby at her breast and have no compassion on the child she has borne...I will not forget you!" says the Lord (Isaiah 49:15). You have become an adulteress, but I want you back (Hosea 3:1). I will rejoice over you as a husband over a bride (Isaiah 62:5). I am jealous for you (Deuteronomy 4:24). "I am burning with jealousy for [you]" (Zechariah 8:2). It is too easy to focus on the violence that was in the Old Testament and miss the great affection of God for his people. "Comfort, comfort my people, says your God. Speak tenderly to Jerusalem" (Isaiah 40:1-2). "All day long I have held out my hands" (Isaiah 65:2).

How else could God show us his love? How could God convince us once and for all?

> In the past God spoke to our forefathers through the prophets at many times and in various ways, but in these last days he has spoken to us by his Son, whom he appointed heir of all things, and through whom he made the universe. The Son is the radiance of God's glory and the exact representation of his being, sustaining all things by his powerful word. After he had provided purification for sins, he sat down at the right hand of the Majesty in heaven. (Hebrews 1:1-3)

In Christ, God entered, invaded, our little planet. He wrapped himself with flesh and showed us his glory. Christ is the Word made flesh. To see him is to see God. He is the fullness of the Godhead and in him is the Spirit without limit (John 3:34). How does God love us? Let me count the ways through Jesus.

PERSONAL TOUCH

In Jesus, God could be touched. The holy one of Israel—who dwelt in the temple in glory, who would kill those who simply touched or even looked at the ark (1 Samuel 6:19)—allowed people on the earth to touch more than just the ark. Men touched God and lived.

> That which was from the beginning, which we have heard,
> which we have seen with our eyes, which we have looked at
> and our hands have touched—this we proclaim concerning
> the Word of life. (1 John 1:1)

Jesus also touched us, reaching out to individual lives, healing them physically and spiritually. He touched lepers with his hands when he could have healed them with a word (Matthew 8:2-3, Mark 1:40-42, Luke 5:12-13). He stopped a citywide parade because of one blind beggar (Mark 10:46-52). He put a Samaritan woman's cup to his lips (John 4:4-10). He had lunch at a tax collector's house (Luke 19:1-10). Jesus was the kind of man who would use your comb, your towel and your bed. The crowds didn't know what to make of this kind of Messiah, this kind of Savior. As usual, the crowd is almost always wrong about God. And they were wrong about Jesus too.

Jesus was approachable. For example, a sinful woman once burst into a large gathering of the religious elite to get to him (Luke 7:36-50). She *knew* they despised her, but she also knew Jesus would love and accept her. Can you imagine how embarrassing, how devastating it would have been for her if Jesus had pulled back even a little or winced in apprehension or responded awkwardly?

Jesus' love was so magnetic, so divine. He was *so* approachable that Peter was emboldened to pull him aside and rebuke him, even after calling him the Son of the living God! (See Matthew 16:15-23.)

KEENLY AWARE

Because of his selfless love, Jesus noticed things. A man in a tree (Luke 19:4-5). The voice of a beggar (Mark 10:46-52). The innocence of a child (Matthew 18:1-10). The true intent behind a foolish act (Matthew 26:6-13). The heart behind two small coins (Mark 12:42). The touch of a woman in a crowd (Luke 8:44-48). After he raised a little girl from the dead, he said, "Give her something to eat" (Mark 5:40-43)—nice touch. After he cured a man of his insanity, he put clothes on him (Mark 5:15)—whose clothes, I wonder?

The Son of God was affectionate and tender. He wept at Lazarus' tomb, even when he knew he would raise him from the dead (John 11:35). He wept over the city that would shortly cry out for his blood (Luke 19:41). He was protective of Mary when she washed his feet with her tears (Luke 7:44-50). And he was protective of Peter in the courtyard. If Jesus had even winked, had done anything but look at Peter, Peter would have been taken away as well. But he didn't. Their eyes met, and that look broke Peter's heart (Luke 22:56-62). "A bruised reed he will not break, and a smoldering wick he will not snuff out" (Matthew 12:20).

And Jesus was patient—with everyone. He gave to those who were ungrateful, who wouldn't come back to thank him (Luke 17:12-19). The crowds constantly pressed around him, thousands trampling on one another simply to touch him (Luke 12:1-2), and he would welcome them all.

ULTIMATE, SINLESS LOVE

The One and Only was sinless (Hebrews 4:15). His sinlessness perhaps speaks more than anything else of his true love for us. Not once did he wish ill or have a slanderous thought, a proud thought, a bitter thought or a demeaning thought. Not one word of gossip, flattery or insensitivity. No hesitation to serve. No begrudging those who groped for him. No haughty thought toward those who were dull and hardened. Even when he had to rebuke the Pharisees and call them sons of hell, he did it with a heart full of love (Matthew 23). What surprises us the most about these interactions—his sinlessness or his perfect love?

He washed the feet of twelve men who would shortly abandon and betray him, showing them "the full extent of his love" (John 13:1-12). God on his knees, looking up! After three years or so together, Jesus said, "One of you will betray me" (Matthew 26:21). Did all eyes turn to Judas? No! Not even when Judas left the room did the others suspect him. And why not? Jesus knew from the beginning it was he, but his love for Judas was so pure and perfect, so impartial, that no one else even suspected him.

It was Christ who comforted his apostles before his crucifixion, not the other way around (John 14-17). And after he rose from the dead, he did not utter one word of rebuke. Instead, he prepared a fish breakfast and invited them to touch his hands (John 20:26-21:14). As for Peter, was he made a junior apostle after calling curses on himself and swearing that he didn't know Jesus? No. Peter kept the keys that had been given to him by Jesus (Matthew 16:19), and fifty days later, he was proclaiming the greatness of his Savior (Acts 2).

On the cross, Jesus forgave a thief who, moments before, was heaping insults on him (Matthew 27:44). "Today you will be with me in paradise" (Luke 23:43). Jesus could have either said "Yes" or simply nodded, but even on the cross, he pushed on his crucified feet one more time, filling his lungs with breath so he could speak, enduring even more agony, just to be able to comfort and reassure his newest disciple. "I tell you the truth..." (Luke 23:43). He didn't have to do that, but he did it anyway.

On this bitter tree, surrounded by wild dogs and bulls (Psalm 22:12, 16), the Son of God was slaughtered, disfigured beyond human recognition (Isaiah 52:14). He was cursed (Galatians 3:13), crushed (Isaiah 53:10) and cut off from his Father (Matthew 27:46), but even then, he loved, he gave, he wept. In the midst of all this darkness, to the cadence of hammering nails, we hear the cry of his beating heart, "Father, forgive them."

My Father, Your Father

Once when he spoke of God his Father, it was with the image of an older man running, perhaps stumbling, toward the son who had violated his honor.

> "Bring the best robe and put it on him. Put a ring on his finger and sandals on his feet. Bring the fattened calf and kill it. Let's have a feast and celebrate." (Luke 15:22-23)

The son didn't even have a chance to finish his apology. This is your God, taught Jesus: a God who runs. In the words of an old poem,

Whoso draws nigh to God through doubtings dim
God will advance a mile in blazing light to him.[1]

A God who runs. A God who weeps. A God who dies. So divine: "Father, forgive them" (Luke 23:34). So humble: "on a donkey" (Matthew 21:5). So approachable: "[John] leaned back against Jesus at the supper" (John 21:20). So tender: "She has done a beautiful thing to me" (Matthew 26:10). So compassionate: "Don't cry" (Luke 7:13). So willing: "Who touched me?" (Luke 8:45). So thoughtful: "Dear woman, here is your son" (John 19:26). So selfless: "I am thirsty"—spoken only after his mission was complete (John 19:28). So vulnerable: "He was led like a lamb to the slaughter" (Isaiah 53:7). So human: "They spit on him" (Matthew 27:30). A love so utterly complete, utterly real, utterly desperate for a relationship with us: "There they crucified him" (Luke 23:33).

How else can God say it? How else can God show it? His love is not a mathematical formula or a cold syllogism: "God loved the world. I'm a part of the world, therefore God loves me." No, No, NO! God's love is fully focused on each and every one of us. He cannot do otherwise. He is God. He is your God. God is love.

This is the God we approach in worship. This should give our hearts great rest and peace. This should endear God to us and enable us to be confident before the throne of grace. We have a high priest who is merciful. Jesus lives to intercede for us. When we come to the Father, we may call him *Abba,* even as his beloved son called him *Abba.* But there is more—"God has poured out his love into our hearts by the Holy Spirit, whom he has given us" (Romans 5:5)—which, if you think about it, is like standing directly under Niagara Falls with a little cup in our hands. God doesn't just satisfy us with love; God buries us with love.

---

[1] Author unknown.

7

RIVER OF FIRE

A RIVER OF FIRE WAS FLOWING,
　　COMING OUT FROM BEFORE HIM.
THOUSANDS UPON THOUSANDS ATTENDED HIM;
　　TEN THOUSAND TIMES TEN THOUSAND STOOD BEFORE
　　　　HIM.
THE COURT WAS SEATED,
　　AND THE BOOKS WERE OPENED.
　　　　　　　　　　　　　　DANIEL 7:10

Would you offer your child as a blood sacrifice and burnt offering? Why did Abraham?

> Now I know that you fear God, because you have not withheld from me your son, your only son." (Genesis 22:12, emphasis mine)

Is it any wonder God was called "the Fear of Isaac"? (See Genesis 31:42.)

Would you build a boat for years, without seeing rain, becoming a laughingstock to all mankind, with only a word of warning? Why did Noah?

> In holy fear [he] built an ark to save his family. By his faith he condemned the world. (Hebrews 11:7, emphasis mine)

Our fear is a holy fear, and our confident expectation is for mercy and grace, not the horrors of condemnation. But there is an altogether different fear for the unrepentant—believers and unbelievers alike—"a fearful expectation of judgment and of raging fire that will consume the enemies of God" (Hebrews 10:26-27). Paul describes the Day of Judgment simply as "the coming wrath" (1 Thessalonians 1:10). Indeed, "It is a dreadful thing to fall into the hands of the living God" (Hebrews 10:31).

Too often, I have heard people trying to minimize this fear of God, saying it is mere reverence or healthy respect, like that given by a child to her father or a slave to his master. I strongly disagree. To be sure, we need to approach God with absolute reverence and respect (Malachi 1). But it goes beyond this and includes some rather bitter truths we must grapple with. Certainly God wants his saints to regard his fearsomeness differently than unrepentant sinners do. However, how each of us responds to the Fear, the Consuming Fire, will determine whether we live or die.

Fire is useful or harmful. We can use it for warmth, light or cooking—even romance—or we can foolishly play with it and burn the house down. The fear of God is the same—blessing or curse, life or death, wonderful light or consuming fire. All of us are given choices: to believe or not believe; to be serious about the things of God or sloppy and sentimental; to choose care and caution over carelessness. Joy and laughter are appropriate at times, of course (Psalm 126:2). But should we ever be complacent, irreverent, flippant or unafraid, before the one who hates sin with a violent hatred?

God's throne is a throne of grace, but it is also "a river of fire" (Daniel 7:10). God cautioned his people, "The Light of Israel will become a fire, their Holy One a flame" (Isaiah 10:17), and again, "The LORD Almighty is the one you are to regard as holy, he is the one you are to fear, he is the one you are to dread" (Isaiah 8:13).

Usually, when I begin an exhaustive study of a subject, I buy a new Bible and mark the references pertaining only to my subject. For instance, I have one Bible that I have used to study out the attributes of God (that one is fully marked), another for a study on heaven, still another that I have used for this book about worship. I also have a Bible dedicated to the fear of God. Here are a few of the points I learned from that study, and I hope they will impress you as they did me.

Fear Is a Gift

Consider these scriptures about fearing God. "Those who fear [God] lack nothing" (Psalm 34:9). "The fear of the Lord is the beginning of wisdom" (Proverbs 9:10). "The fear of the Lord is a fountain of life" (Proverbs 14:27). "The Lord delights in those who fear him" (Psalm 147:11). "Through the fear of the Lord a man avoids evil" (Proverbs 16:6). The point is that fear of God saves lives. It is the single key to a great and precious treasure (Isaiah 33:6).

The fear of God is a grace. God said that he would himself soften his people's hearts and inspire them to fear him (Ezekiel 36:26). "'Twas grace that taught my heart to fear...." In other words, even the ability to fear God is itself a gift from God, an act of grace, a reward from heaven.

> My son, if you accept my words
>   and store up my commands within you,
> turning your ear to wisdom
>   and applying your heart to understanding,
> and if you call out for insight
>   and cry aloud for understanding,
> and if you look for it as for silver
>   and search for it as for hidden treasure,
> then you will understand the fear of the Lord
>   and find the knowledge of God. (Proverbs 2:1-5)

The fear of God is supremely the ability to see God for who he is. Great and fiery, awesome in judgment, holy and mysterious—not the idol we want him to be. For example, the purpose of Mount Sinai's terrors was to keep the Israelites from sinning. Fear saves us. It makes us revere God. It makes us take his word seriously. It makes us approach him with deliberation and caution as well as with the joyful confidence he wants us to have. John the Baptist said concerning Jesus,

> "His winnowing fork is in his hand to clear his threshing floor
> and to gather the wheat into his barn, but he will burn up the
> chaff with unquenchable fire." And with many other words,
> John exhorted the people and preached the good news to
> them. (Luke 3:17-18)

If a message of judgment keeps us close to God and away from sin, it is indeed good news!

On a personal note, I made my decision to become a Christian after reading the book of Revelation. I had read through the rest of the New Testament and had begun to fall in love with Jesus. This was my first time reading the Bible, and I understood so little. In fact, I understood almost nothing about the book of Revelation; but as I began to read it, I got the main point: God's team is the winning team, and I was on the losing side. More than that, I could not escape feeling that I was caught in the midst of a heart-pounding horror story. Shortly afterward, I was baptized.

Mysteriously, without question or hesitation, God loves those whom he punishes—but punish he must. The Bible says that God is not willing that any should perish and that he wants all men to be saved (2 Peter 3:9, 1 Timothy 2:4). He forgave those who insulted him (Luke 23:34). In his mercy, he gives us time to repent (Romans 2:4, Revelation 2 and 3).

God wanted to save even the most wicked of nations, the Assyrians. The Assyrians would choke rivers with the bones and bodies of their victims. They would wallpaper the temples of their gods with the flayed skin of rival monarchs. They would drag captives for miles with hooks in their flesh. It was a brutal and savage nation. But God loved them, and on this matter Jonah was rebuked (Jonah 4:9-11). In fact, God judges everyone who wants him to destroy others, who delight in calamity. God is desperate to save us. He will go to any length and pay any price, including the giving of his Son.

A very poignant passage in Genesis reveals that "[God's] heart was filled with pain" (Genesis 6:6). He resists having to judge and destroy for as long as he can. Sometimes, judgment is instantaneous; other times it may take hundreds of years, as with the Amorites (Genesis 15:16). But judge he must, because he is a holy God who abhors sin. Sin and rebellion are extremely offensive to him. Idolatry is repulsive and dangerous, which is why the Israelites were sometimes commanded to kill everything that breathed as they conquered various nations. God wanted no trace of idolatry left, not even on the lips of infants.

At the same time, God anguishes over those he must destroy. The sight is pitiful, even embarrassing to God. "All day long I have held out my hands to a disobedient and obstinate people" (Romans 10:21). He sent his prophets again and again, but the people would not listen.

Jesus wept over Jerusalem,

> "O Jerusalem, Jerusalem, you who kill the prophets and stone those sent to you, how often I have longed to gather your children together, as a hen gathers her chicks under her wings, but you were not willing." (Matthew 23:37)

Even on his way to his crucifixion he said, "Do not weep for me; weep for yourselves and for your children" (Luke 23:28). God sent his Son to be our Savior, a title that begs the question: Savior from what? From the coming wrath, from eternal destruction, from the wages of sin.

CALCULATED TO TERRIFY

Fear means fear. Dread means dread. Terror means terror. Horror means horror. The Bible is its own best interpreter. Consider these descriptions: Men will "shudder with fear" (Isaiah 19:16) and "every hand will go limp, and every knee will become as weak as water" (Ezekiel 7:17); not to mention that

> ...every man's heart will melt.
> Terror will seize them,
>   pain and anguish will grip them;
>   they will writhe like a woman in labor.
> They will look aghast at each other,
>   their faces aflame. (Isaiah 13:7-8)

As the psalmist declared, "For your wrath is as great as the fear that is due you" (Psalm 90:11). Understand God's wrath, and you will understand perfectly the depth and meaning that this fear of God evokes.

"The understanding of this message will bring sheer terror" (Isaiah 28:19). This was the goal of God's word through Isaiah, and this is part of the goal of his word today. When the Israelites stood at the foot of Mount Sinai to meet God, they were terrified. (See Exodus 19:16-19.) "The sight was so terrifying that Moses said, 'I am trembling with fear'" (Hebrews 12:21). What was the purpose of this fear?

> Moses said to the people, "Do not be afraid. God has come to test you, so that the fear of God will be with you to keep you from sinning." (Exodus 20:20)

God wanted to terrify them to keep them from sinning. *This was the point.* When Ananias and Sapphira were struck dead, Luke notes that "great fear seized the whole church" (Acts 5:11). Again, *this was the point!*

The judgments exacted by God and the images they convey are meant to melt our hearts with fear. This is their express purpose. Throughout the Bible, terrifying imagery is used to describe the fate of the wicked.

> So beware, the days are coming, declares the LORD, when people will no longer call it Topheth or the Valley of Ben Hinnom, but the Valley of Slaughter, for they will bury the dead in Topheth until there is no more room. (Jeremiah 7:32)

> "Jezebel's body will be like refuse on the ground in the plot at Jezreel, so that no one will be able to say, 'This is Jezebel.'" (2 Kings 9:37)

> I will bring distress on the people
>   and they will walk like blind men,
>   because they have sinned against the LORD.
> Their blood will be poured out like dust
>   and their entrails like filth. (Zephaniah 1:17)

> I will pull up your skirts over your face
>   that your shame may be seen. (Jeremiah 13:26)

"I will pelt you with filth,
    I will treat you with contempt
    and make you a spectacle." (Nahum 3:6)

Drag them off like sheep to be butchered!
    Set them apart for the day of slaughter! (Jeremiah 12:3)

Their infants will be dashed to pieces before their eyes;
    their houses will be looted and their wives ravished.
(Isaiah 13:16)

These men are springs without water and mists driven by a
storm. Blackest darkness is reserved for them. (2 Peter 2:17)

God will stretch out over Edom
    the measuring line of chaos
    and the plumb line of desolation. (Isaiah 34:11)

The Lord Almighty will lash them with a whip,
    as when he struck down Midian at the rock of Oreb.
(Isaiah 10:26)

But that day belongs to the Lord, the Lord Almighty—
    a day of vengeance, for vengeance on his foes.
The sword will devour till it is satisfied,
    till it has quenched its thirst with blood. (Jeremiah 46:10)

Risk of Caricature

God describes himself in ways that are simply shocking to the heart.
His anger is terrifying. He describes his anger in ways that seem
frighteningly human, not divine: "I was enraged" (Isaiah 57:17), "in a
surge of anger" (Isaiah 54:8), "his wrath can flare up in a moment"
(Psalm 2:12), "fierce anger" (Numbers 25:4), "dreadful" (Joel 2:31) and
"cruel" (Isaiah 13:9). He is willing to risk misunderstanding, even
regarding his character, if this is what is needed to get through to us.
These are not images we want our children to think about often, let
alone ourselves. To the hardened and unbelieving, this is nothing more

than caricature and "slaughterhouse religion." Listen to God's response to the question, "Why are your garments red?"

> "I have trodden the winepress alone;
>   from the nations no one was with me.
> I trampled them in my anger
>   and trod them down in my wrath;
> their blood spattered my garments,
>   and I stained all my clothing.
> For the day of vengeance was in my heart,
>   and the year of my redemption has come."
> (Isaiah 63:3-4)

But you may say, "Things are different with Jesus." And the Bible answers with this:

> He said in a loud voice, "Fear God and give him glory, because the hour of his judgment has come. Worship him who made the heavens, the earth, the sea and the springs of water."
> …"He, too, will drink of the wine of God's fury, which has been poured full strength into the cup of his wrath. He will be tormented with burning sulfur in the presence of the holy angels *and of the Lamb*. And the smoke of their torment rises for ever and ever. There is no rest day or night for those who worship the beast and his image, or for anyone who receives the mark of his name." (Revelation 14:7, 10-11, emphasis mine)

When men are cast into hell, Christ himself will do it.

> "Then he will say to those on his left, 'Depart from me, you who are cursed, into the eternal fire prepared for the devil and his angels.'" (Matthew 25:41)

Think clearly here. If hell is the just punishment for Satan, the one who has led the whole world astray and fallen angels into rebellion against God, how unimaginably horrifying it must be! How evil sin must be. Do we truly fear, as Jonathan Edwards did, the fate of "sinners in the hands of an angry God"? The Hebrew writer warns, "It is a dreadful thing to fall into the hands of the living God" (Hebrews 10:31).

No Apologies Given

The Bible offers no apologies or tempering, no "Please don't misunderstand what I'm about to say" or "This is just poetry." We, on the other hand, take pains to make sure people understand the "balance" of God's character: "Yes, he is angry; yes, he is holy; but he is so loving." This is well and good, for it takes into account the whole counsel of God. However, it amazes me that neither God nor Christ made any apologies whatsoever for these descriptions. There is no special buildup to prepare us. Consider, after many years of silence, the very first words in the prophecy of Zephaniah:

> "I will sweep away everything
>   from the face of the earth,"
>   declares the LORD.
> "I will sweep away both men and animals;
>   I will sweep away the birds of the air
>   and the fish of the sea.
> The wicked will have only heaps of rubble
>   when I cut off man from the face of the earth,"
>   declares the LORD. (Zephaniah 1:2-3)

No attempt is made to protect the sensitive among us, no effort to hide them even from children (Joel 2:15-16). God's judgments on Uzzah (2 Samuel 6:1-8) and on Nadab and Abihu (Leviticus 10:1-5) were severe and immediate. In response, "Aaron remained silent" (Leviticus 10:3) and "David was afraid of the LORD that day" (2 Samuel 6:9). Refusing to submit to God's leadership, Korah, Dathan and Abiram— and their families—were swallowed alive by the earth, and fire from the Lord consumed 250 men (Numbers 16). The only things that were not consumed in this fiery destruction were the temple utensils. These censers were a sign for Israel, a daily reminder to approach the holy God with holy fear.

MAKING AN APPEAL

In order to get everyone's attention, God appeals to all kinds of temperaments, imaginations and fears. What may not put a knot in your stomach will surely horrify someone else. Name your phobias. Are you frightened by the thought of dead bodies eaten by vultures, banishment into darkness, or miles and miles of blood? Do you fear the assault or murder of loved ones, eternal fire or unending torment?

> See, the day of the LORD is coming
> —a cruel day, with wrath and fierce anger—
> to make the land desolate
> and destroy the sinners within it. (Isaiah 13:9)

Are you afraid of evil men?

> I will hand you over to brutal men,
> men skilled in destruction. (Ezekiel 21:31)

Are you afraid of prison? You will be imprisoned not just with evil people, but with the evil one. And if these things don't bother you, "the sword you fear *will* overtake you" (Jeremiah 42:16, emphasis mine).

GOD'S WRATH IS PERSONAL

Robed in fierce anger, God once said of his judgments: "my own wrath sustained me" (Isaiah 63:5). This wrath is not some impersonal force or some evil gone out of control or merely bad men doing bad things. God's judgments are personal, and he takes pains to let us know that he is behind them, that he is the architect and death-bringer. "It is I who have created the destroyer to work havoc" (Isaiah 54:16). "I will bring you to a horrible end" (Ezekiel 26:21).

> "You have rejected me," declares the LORD.
> "You keep on backsliding.
> So I will lay hands on you and destroy you;
> I can no longer show compassion.
> I will winnow them with a winnowing fork
> at the city gates of the land.

I will bring bereavement and destruction on my people,
 for they have not changed their ways.
I will make their widows more numerous
 than the sand of the sea.
At midday I will bring a destroyer
 against the mothers of their young men;
suddenly I will bring down on them
 anguish and terror.
The mother of seven will grow faint
 and breathe her last.
Her sun will set while it is still day;
 she will be disgraced and humiliated.
I will put the survivors to the sword
 before their enemies,"
  declares the Lord. (Jeremiah 15:6-9)

This is what the Lord Almighty says:

"See, I will break the bow of Elam,
 the mainstay of their might.
I will bring against Elam the four winds
 from the four quarters of the heavens;
I will scatter them to the four winds,
 and there will not be a nation
 where Elam's exiles do not go.
I will shatter Elam before their foes,
 before those who seek their lives;
I will bring disaster upon them,
 even my fierce anger,"
 declares the Lord.
"I will pursue them with the sword
 until I have made an end of them.
I will set my throne in Elam
 and destroy her king and officials,"
  declares the Lord. (Jeremiah 49:35-38)

"I will spread your flesh on the mountains
 and fill the valleys with your remains.
I will drench the land with your flowing blood
 all the way to the mountains,
 and the ravines will be filled with your flesh.

> When I snuff you out, I will cover the heavens
>> and darken their stars;
> I will cover the sun with a cloud,
>> and the moon will not give its light." (Ezekiel 32:5-7)

> "I sent plagues among you
>> as I did to Egypt.
> I killed your young men with the sword,
>> along with your captured horses.
> I filled your nostrils with the stench of your camps,
>> yet you have not returned to me,"
>>> declares the LORD. (Amos 4:10)

NEVER TRIFLE WITH GOD

We must never take God for a fool. He means what he says. David gathered thousands of dignitaries from all over Israel. He was planning the parade of all parades, the celebration of all celebrations. The ark of God was returning to Jerusalem! They placed the ark on a brand new cart—only this would do. They sang and danced and "celebrated with all their might" (2 Samuel 6:5), with David leading the way. Suddenly, the oxen stumbled and the ark of God's might, "his splendor," was about to fall to the ground and perhaps break to pieces. Perhaps Uzzah's life flashed before his eyes and he thought, *Who could forgive me? I'll be written up by the prophets: "Uzzah stood by and did nothing." Or they will sing songs about me: "Uzzah was banished, away from his God, like wandering Cain in the desert of Nod."* So, what did he do? He reached out his hand to steady the ark...to do God a favor, I suppose. Of course, five hundred years earlier, God had commanded that no hand should touch the ark and that only Levites were to carry it (Numbers 1:50-51). Uzzah was struck dead and the party was over.

Nadab and Abihu, sons of Aaron, were killed on the first day of their new job. Zedekiah's sons were slaughtered before his eyes and then the Babylonians gouged his own eyes out. For the rest of his life, the last image he would recall was the killing of his children. God disciplined

Israel through the exile and destruction of Jerusalem, even though it meant the desecration of his own temple and name (Psalm 74). He allowed himself to be blasphemed to punish the sin of his people. And he will one day judge the world for its rejection of Jesus Christ. God has indeed demonstrated his love, but he has also demonstrated his wrath. God is serious.

What does God want us to see from all this? He wants us to know that whatever it takes, we need to get right with him, we need to revere him. In the Sermon on the Mount, Jesus said to cut your hand off, gouge your eye out and even throw it away if it causes you to sin. In other words, do anything rather than go to hell. We are told to "make every effort...to be holy," because "without holiness, no one will see the Lord" (Hebrews 12:14). We are to "work out [our] salvation with fear and trembling" (Philippians 2:12). We are told to remember Esau, "who for a single meal sold his inheritance rights as the oldest son," and who could not change the situation, not even with tears (Hebrews 12:16-17).

Like the prophet said, "the understanding of this message will bring sheer terror" (Isaiah 28:19). But for us who have been called and who love God, these words serve as a warning to keep us on the straight and narrow. They teach us to walk humbly before God with reverence and awe. They help us to guard our hearts and keep us from being careless or casual before Almighty God. "God is in heaven and you are on earth, so let your words be few.... Therefore, stand in awe of God" (Ecclesiastes 5:2, 7).

APPROACHING GOD

How shall we think of God in worship? He is "the Blessed One" (Mark 14:61) and "the One to be feared" (Psalm 76:11). He is transcendent, above and beyond his creation, and he is imminent, involved and near and throughout his creation. He fills the heavens, and he fills our hearts as well.

For the elect, he is our *Abba*, Father. We are true sons and daughters. His throne is a gracious throne. God desires our love, wants our love, and deserves our love. He doesn't want us to fear him in a way that damages our intimacy or enjoyment and belief in his mercy. Our covenant is a life-bringing covenant of grace and truth.

On the other hand, God is a consuming fire, especially toward his enemies. His love and holiness cannot be separated. He is good and kind and loving always, but he is also holy and righteous and fiery always. One does not exclude the other. One does not diminish the other.

We are not supposed to be schizophrenic in our approach to God, but at peace—with a peace that passes understanding (Philippians 4:7). The child of an abusive parent must constantly wonder, "Will he embrace me or beat me? Will she hit me or hug me?" This child must walk on eggshells, and he or she is crippled emotionally by the erratic behavior of the parent. God is nothing like this at all, and I am embarrassed to use this analogy; but the truth is, because of our backgrounds, some of us project these feelings onto God. This is why we should focus on God's mercy—but a "mercy mixed with fear" (Jude 23). As we worship, we need to remember both of these aspects of God's nature.

> Serve the LORD with fear
>   and rejoice with trembling. (Psalm 2:11)

The early church was "encouraged by the Holy Spirit...living in the fear of the Lord" (Acts 9:31). Together with them,

> ...let us be thankful, and so worship God acceptably with reverence and awe, for our "God is a consuming fire." (Hebrews 12:28-29)

8

CHRIST ALL, CHRIST ONLY

If I had a thousand heads and each head had a thousand tongues and each tongue spoke a thousand dialects and I could speak for eternity, I still would not praise Jesus sufficiently.

ROBERT G. LEE

Christ is the aperture through which the immensity and magnificence of God can be seen.

J. B. PHILLIPS

A while back I made a discovery that opened my eyes in a remarkable way. The discovery had to do with who Jesus Christ is and about his place and prominence in my life and ministry. Nothing new, really—but so much clearer than before. In fact, I believed these things and preached them, but had never fully grasped their significance. Their depth and breathtaking simplicity escaped me. My discovery was simply this: Christ is all, and Christ is in all. To quote J. B. Phillips, "Christ is all that matters" (Colossians 3:11). Jesus is the center of the center of the center of all things. In his own words,

> "Now this is eternal life: that they may know you, the only true God, and Jesus Christ, whom you have sent." (John 17:3)

I now realize that the pearl of great price is not about me or my salvation, but about a person, Jesus Christ. He is the key to heaven and earth. He is the centerpiece of heaven, the crown of all creation, the reason paradise is paradise. I know that you know this; but something wonderful happened, at least for me, when I really got it. The beginning of my new way of seeing started as I read the first chapter of 1 Corinthians (specifically verses 1-18). Take a moment to read it right now and as you do so, stand amazed at how Christ is woven into almost every thought, every truth, every motive and every longing of Paul. Please take the time right now to read it—it's that important!

The emphasis on Christ in this passage is stunning. It is so simple, so obvious, so right—but it caught me completely off guard. What is the Holy Spirit trying to teach us here? Are we supposed to be impressed with the richness of Paul's relationship with Jesus, to be humbled by his spirituality? Or is this a call to a deeper understanding of who Jesus is and the need to let thoughts of Christ saturate our religious life, our entire life?

Imagine how we would sound if every sentence or two we mentioned something about Jesus. We'd be considered religious fanatics, even among our own number! I'm not saying that's how we're supposed to talk. But surely it is how we're supposed to think. Every thought taken captive by Christ (2 Corinthians 10:5). Every word and deed for Christ. Every bite and swallow for Christ. Every ambition and motive for Christ. Jesus is not the most important aspect of our lives, he *is* our life—above and below, in us and through us, all and only, now and forever.

HIS NAME IS WONDERFUL

Who is Jesus Christ? Words are paltry, but words are all we have. How do we communicate the glory and fullness of his life and grace? "Wonderful" (Isaiah 9:6)—who can express it? He was born of a virgin (Isaiah 7:14)—who can grasp it? He was "without sin," the "Holy One of God" (Hebrews 4:15, John 6:69)—who can relate to it? "You killed the author of life" (Acts 3:15)—who can remotely fathom it? He became sin for us (2 Corinthians 5:21)—who can believe it? Indeed, if these things were not true, who *could* believe it? The reason we are able to worship God at all, the reason we are alive and not dead, the reason we love one another, the reason we know God and what God truly is like is Jesus Christ.

He is God and man, flesh and spirit, Lion and Lamb. He is King and servant, meekness and majesty. He is fully human, like us in every way. "Since the children have flesh and blood, he too shared in their humanity" (Hebrews 2:14). And he is God: the Word of God "became flesh" and lived for awhile among us (John 1:14).

We are to fix our eyes on him, to remember him, to imitate him, to do all things for him and through him, because apart from him, we can do nothing. We must set our "hearts on things above, where Christ is seated at the right hand of God" (Colossians 3:1). He is our life, and so inextricably so, that when he appears, we shall "appear with him in glory" (Colossians 3:4). He is to be lifted up, prayed to, preached and worshiped.[1]

Jesus Christ fills the universe. He has "ascended higher than all the heavens, in order to fill the whole universe" (Ephesians 4:10). He is "set apart from sinners, exalted above the heavens" (Hebrews 7:26). He is "the fullness of him who fills everything in every way" (Ephesians 1:23). He is "the bright Morning Star" (Revelation 22:16), glorious and beautiful, and "the desire of all nations" (Haggai 2:7 KJV). Christ is the one and only Son of God (1 John 4:9), the Word made flesh. He is the incarnation of love, the full contents and expression of God (Colossians 2:9). "He is before all things, and in him all things hold together" (Colossians 1:17). "Whether thrones or powers or rulers or authorities," visible or invisible, "all things were created by him and for him" (Colossians 1:16). He is "the radiance of God's glory and the *exact* representation of his being, sustaining all things by his powerful word" (Hebrews 1:3, emphasis mine). He reigns in majesty with grace and terrifying greatness. He is the embodiment of moral perfection, the sum of all excellence, the epitome of beauty. He is the Lord of creation and the servant of creation. In him are "*all* the treasures of wisdom and knowledge" (Colossians 2:3, emphasis mine). The fullness of deity, of the Godhead, dwells within him. He is "perfect forever" (Hebrews 7:28).

---

[1] Many scriptures are woven throughout this chapter. Enjoy the search!

LIFE TO THE FULL

"In him was life" (John 1:4). His words are life (John 6:63). He is our life (Colossians 3:4). He is called the "author of life" (Acts 3:15) and "the eternal life, which was with the Father" (1 John 1:2). He is "the hope of glory" (Colossians 1:27), the "firstborn over all creation" (Colossians 1:15) and the "firstborn among many brothers" (Romans 8:29). Even now he stands in the presence of God on our behalf (1 John 2:1). He lives "to intercede for [us]" (Hebrews 7:25), and we have access to our Father through him (John 14:6). Because of his eternal love for Christ (John 17:24), God desires that his Son be the crowning jewel of all creation—and this is what he is (Ephesians 1:20-21). Our worship is our expression of this.

To see Christ is to see the Father (John 14:9). To honor the Son is to honor the Father (John 5:23). And it is the Spirit of the Godhead who has made all this known to us (Ephesians 3:5). We gather on the Lord's Day and assemble in his name. We take the Lord's Supper. We remember his body and his blood (1 Corinthians 11:24-25). We participate in these things, through his blood that was shed for us (1 Corinthians 10:16). We pray in his name (John 14:14) and preach his gospel (Romans 15:19). His word dwells richly within us, and from this richness, we are to sing to one another (Colossians 3:16). His Spirit is placed in our bodies (1 Corinthians 3:16), and his gifts have been given to each and every one of us (1 Corinthians 12:4, Ephesians 4:10-11).

He has purchased us (Acts 20:28, Revelation 5:9). He has redeemed us (1 Peter 1:18-19). And all "power and wealth and wisdom and strength and honor and glory and praise" belong to him (Revelation 5:12). Christ has "all authority in heaven and on earth" (Matthew 28:18). All things are under his feet, all things serve him, and he sustains and rules all things. He is exalted to the highest place and is above every name and title that can be given (Philippians 2:9-11), "far above all rule and authority, power and dominion...not only in the present age but also in the one to come" (Ephesians 1:21). When he speaks, all of the dead in the history of mankind will rise to face him (John 5:28).

He is Son of David, son of Mary, son of Abraham, Son of Man, Son of God. He is God, mighty God, Almighty God. He is the servant. He is the king. He is the Lion (Revelation 5:5). He is the Lamb (Revelation 5:8). He is the mystery hidden in God for ages but "now disclosed to the saints" (Colossians 1:26). He is the source, the center, the reason, the joy, the crown and the glory and the end of all things. He is the hymn of all creation.

> For to us a child is born,
>   to us a son is given,
>   and the government will be on his shoulders.
> And he will be called
>   Wonderful Counselor, Mighty God,
>   Everlasting Father, Prince of Peace. (Isaiah 9:6)

> In a loud voice they sang:

> "Worthy is the Lamb, who was slain,
> to receive power and wealth and wisdom and strength
> and honor and glory and praise!" (Revelation 5:12)

He is the Beginning and the End, the First and the Last, the Alpha and the Omega (Revelation 22:13). In his hands he holds the keys of life and death (Revelation 1:18). He is the same yesterday, today and forever (Hebrews 13:8). He is our wisdom, our Redeemer, our holiness, and our mediator. He is our Lord and Savior (2 Peter 3:18).

He is the Someone of all history, and the Someone of all Scripture—someone is coming (OT), someone has come (the Gospels), someone is coming again (NT). He is "the author and perfecter of our faith" (Hebrews12:2). Through him we exist (Hebrews 2:10). The Spirit he sent convicts us of sin (John 16:8, Acts 2:33) and his gospel saves us (Romans 1:16).

We are buried with him and raised with him (Colossians 2:12). We are immersed into him and clothed with him (Galatians 3:27). We have been crucified with him (Galatians 2:20), made alive with him (Ephesians 2:5), united with him (Romans 6:5) and seated with him, even now, in the heavenly realms (Ephesians 1:3, 20; 2:6; 3:10; 6:12). "You died," says Paul, "and your life is now hidden with Christ in God" (Colossians 3:3). His own hands circumcised our sinful natures in baptism (Colossians 2:11-12). His own blood washes us (Hebrews 9:14). "By one sacrifice he has made perfect forever those who are being made holy" (Hebrews 10:14). We are the church of Christ, built on the foundation of Christ and the word of Christ (John 12:48, 1 Corinthians 3:11). He is the chief cornerstone and the living Stone (Ephesians 2:20; 1 Peter 2:4). We are "his body, the fullness of him who fills everything in every way" (Ephesians 1:23). His covenant is better, newer, greater, higher and more honorable. His blood is more precious, more life-giving. He is the center of heaven and earth, the bridge between God and man, fully God and fully man in one person—the man, Christ Jesus.

He is our substitute. He is our treasure. He is our revelation. He is our mediator—crucified between two men, between two covenants, between earth and sky, between heaven and hell.

"From the fullness of his grace we have all received one blessing after another" (John 1:16). He is the "indescribable gift" (2 Corinthians 9:15), the unsearchable gift (Ephesians 3:8), the eternal gift (Romans 6:23). He is our husband (Isaiah 54:5) and we are his bride, the "wife of the Lamb" (Revelation 21:9). He is our co-heir and counterpart in paradise (Romans 8:17). We shall reign with him on his throne (Revelation 3:21). He is the sacrifice and high priest in one person (Hebrews 10:19-22). He is the Lamb and the Lord in one person. He is the Creator and Redeemer in one person.

RIGHT ANSWER

He is the answer to every question and the satisfier of every need (Philippians 4:19). He is bread (John 6:35). He is water (John 4:10). He is shepherd (John 10:11). He is light (John 8:12) and the nourishing vine (John 15:1-2). He is the way, the truth and the life (John 14:6)—the key and the gate to paradise. He is "the resurrection and the life" (John 11:25). To believe in him is to *never* die (John 11:26).

Christ is the word of God—the final word and the fullest expression of God in heaven and on earth. Who touches that leper? God does. Who washes those feet? God does. Who weeps over Jerusalem? God does. Who dies on that cross? God does. "You killed," proclaimed Peter, "the author of life" (Acts 3:15). He is love. He is approachable. He is gracious. He is kind. He is merciful. He is in all and over all—through us, with us and for us. Christ is all and is in all.

He is "gentle and riding on a donkey" (Matthew 21:5). He is awesome and "coming on the clouds of heaven" (Matthew 26:64). He is the "light" and "glory" and "temple" of heaven itself. At his name "every knee [shall] bow... and every tongue confess that Jesus Christ is Lord, to the glory of God the Father" (Philippians 2:10-11).

He is the "King of kings and Lord of lords (1 Timothy 6:15), the "faithful witness" (Revelation 1:5), the "ruler of God's creation" (Revelation 3:14). His eyes are blazing fire, and he walks among the lampstands, the churches. He is the center, the fullness, the richness, the coming and the accomplishment of God's eternal purpose (Ephesians 3:11). Through him, his body and blood, God has reconciled all of creation to himself (Colossians 1:15-23). In him all things in heaven and on earth will come "together under one head, even Christ" (Ephesians 1:10). He is the sum of all being, the cause and final goal of the entire universe. All honor has been conferred on him. All creation will worship him. He is our victory. He is our advocate. He is the judge of all the earth. He is the Amen of God.

He is the Lamb that was slain, the veil that was torn and the high priest who offers his sinless blood on our behalf—poured, sprinkled, lavished, cleansing, washing, redeeming, purifying blood. Blood so amazing, so divine, so utterly awesome—blood of the eternal covenant that had power to raise Christ from the dead (Hebrews 13:20). Nothing else matters but Christ.

There is no one else but Christ, none other that we must look to. "This is my Son," said the voice from the Majestic Glory. "Listen to him" (Mark 9:7, 2 Peter 1:17). "To whom shall we go?" Only Jesus. "You have the words of eternal life" (John 6:68). There is no other name that saves except Jesus (Acts 4:12). There is but one God and one mediator between God and men—Jesus (1 Timothy 2:5). His love compels us (2 Corinthians 5:14). His life is our message. His Spirit empowers us, directs us (Acts 16:7). In his name we pray and accomplish miracles, and through him alone we have access to the Father. He is our peace (John 16:33). He is our joy. He is our wisdom, our holiness and our redemption (1 Corinthians 1:30).

His love has been poured into our hearts through the Holy Spirit with love so unsearchable that we will never know its height, breadth, width or depth; love so conquering that nothing in all creation can separate us from the love of God that is in Christ Jesus (Romans 8:39). He has loved us with an everlasting love, to the fullest extent, to the laying down of his life.

We can do all things through him (John 14:13). We long for his return. We must exalt him in our bodies by life or by death. We must imitate him and give thanks through him. Through him the world has been crucified to us. He was crucified in weakness, but was raised to the heavens, even the highest heavens. He is our hope of glory, our brother, our beloved and our friend.

He is mystery explained, secrets revealed, paradox made plain and eternal purpose in the brief life of one man. He is the question and he is the answer. He is the gift and he is the giver. Christ became flesh so we could become sons of God. He tasted death for us so we could feast on his life. He became sin for us so that "in him we might become the righteousness of God" (2 Corinthians 5:21). He was born in a stable so we could have homes in heaven. He became nothing so we might become heirs. He was forsaken so we could draw near. He became poor so that we, through his poverty, might become rich. He was a servant so we could be kings. He was crucified so we might be glorified. He was the man of sorrows so we could be filled with an "inexpressible and glorious joy" (1 Peter 1:8). From our creation and call to our conversion, coronation and consummation in heaven, Christ is the center and glory of it all. He is the "author and perfecter of our faith" (Hebrews 12:2). Once again, Christ all, Christ only— the reason, the source, the meaning, the glory, the hope and the hymn of all creation in heaven and on earth, both now and forever. Amen.

Our Turn

How fully can one human being love Jesus? We have only to look at Paul. As David was to the worship of Jehovah, Paul was to the love of Jesus Christ. Christ was Paul's only passion, his only reason for being alive and staying alive (Philippians 1:20-21). Even after visions and encounters, revelations and appearances, and the full understanding he had as an apostle, even after *all this*, what did Paul want? "I want to know Christ and the power of his resurrection and the fellowship of sharing in his sufferings, becoming like him in his death" (Philippians 3:10).

Paul was willing to suffer for him and fill up in his flesh what was "still lacking in regard to Christ's afflictions" (Colossians 1:24). Christ was his strength. Through Christ, he knew that all of his needs would be met. He could do all things through him (Philippians 4:13). Nothing mattered to him "except Jesus Christ and him crucified" (1 Corinthians 2:2). He served God wholeheartedly by "preaching the gospel of [God's] Son" (Romans 1:9). Christ's love compelled Paul (2 Corinthians 5:14) and crucified him to the world (Galatians 6:14).

Like Paul, Mary Magdalene was another great lover of Christ. She simply could not pull away from him. She was deeply in love with Jesus. Her affection was boundless, and she was totally unashamed in her expression of it. She stayed at his feet to listen to him. She returned to worship him and anoint his feet with oil. She cared not for the cost; he was worthy. She cared not about the critics; in fact, she was not even aware of them. She only saw Jesus. Even at the cross, surrounded by God-haters and Christ-killers, she simply could not leave him.

Paul and Mary are tremendous examples of devotion to Jesus. But who is Christ to you and me? What is the normal Christian experience of Jesus supposed to be? Read the New Testament and see for yourself. It is Christ all, Christ only, Christ forever. He must be lifted in our teaching, exemplified to the world, introduced to our children and taught in our classes. He must be the preeminent one in our counseling. It is his life that we imitate, through him that we worship, his supper that we participate in. It is for him that we do what we do. From birth to final consummation in heaven, Christ is everything—the only thing.

> Through Jesus, therefore, let us continually offer to God a sacrifice of praise—the fruit of lips that confess his name. (Hebrews 13:15)

9

Kiss the Son

Serve the Lord with fear
 and rejoice with trembling.
Kiss the Son, lest he be angry
 and you be destroyed in your way,
for his wrath can flare up in a moment.
 Blessed are all who take refuge in him.

Psalm 2:11-12

If anyone does not love the Lord—a curse be on
him. Come, O Lord!

1 Corinthians 16:22

I have had only one dream of the Second Coming. It was quite terrifying. The sky grew metallic, other worldly. The clouds morphed into huge creatures—swift, convulsive and dragonlike. Like a flash of lightning, one of them dived into the ocean and moved like a shark—focused and pulsing, hungry for blood. Its wake was fearful, and a tidal wall formed on both sides. The creature was hidden from sight except for a seething wake of churning water, a mountain that rose above and behind him. Then I woke up. I confessed my sins for the next six hours, examining every inch of my life, reconsecrating myself a hundred times over, and repenting ten times that much. I didn't crack a smile for a week. Of course, the only thing missing in my dream was Jesus.

This wasn't the Second Coming at all. It was more like the breaking of one of the seven seals (Revelation 6-8). Even less than that, it was just a dream, just my imagination. In fact, not one angel is described even remotely like this in the Scriptures. So…what will the coming of our Lord be like? Just a few passages should be enough to evoke our fear and wonder.

ANGELIC HOST

First, let's talk about angels. Angels are powerful, glorious, spiritual beings. They stand before God and are his servants, servants of wind and fire. Seeing an angel with human eyes, in their full splendor, almost always produced terror and agony. Zechariah was gripped with fear. Joshua, the commander of Israel's armies, instinctively bowed with his face to the ground. Daniel was exhausted with trembling. Ezekiel was appalled and overwhelmed. The soldiers at the tomb shook like dead men. Just one angel put to death 185,000 Assyrian soldiers. In Revelation we find that it was Michael and his angels—not Jesus—who cast Satan out of heaven. One angel, sword in hand, stood over Jerusalem ready to smite her because of David's grievous sin. The picture is overwhelming. The apostle John, who instructs us to keep ourselves from idols, twice fell before them to worship.

Each angel is uniquely created by God to serve him. Egypt was decimated by "a band of destroying angels" (Psalm 78:49). In fact, God's agent to kill the firstborn of Egypt was simply called "the destroyer" (Exodus 12:23). In Revelation 9, John explains that "two hundred million" angels were held back, kept waiting for one specific act of judgment—for a particular day and hour; this is why they were created. "I heard their number," said John (Revelation 9:16). The shout of just one angel could be heard throughout the entire creation (Revelation 5:2-3). Yet there are countless billions, if not trillions, of them (Revelation 5:11)—spectacular, powerful, intelligent, sinless beings—totally bent on glorifying God and executing his will.

Why am I saying these things? Because of a tiny three-letter word that can help us understand Christ's coming a little more clearly. It is a word you may have missed before—at least I did.

"When the Son of Man comes in his glory, and *all* the angels with him, he will sit on his throne in heavenly glory." (Matthew 25:31, emphasis mine)

When Jesus comes again, who is coming with him? Angels? Myriads and myriads, thousands upon thousands of angels? Not exactly; how about *all* the angels—every single one! Heaven will be emptied of every last angel. Surrounding their God, swords in hand, ready to act swiftly and decisively, with conviction and the will to kill. They will curse God's enemies and at the same time, gather all those who have longed and hoped for his appearing. They will gather the elect from the four corners of the earth.

Jude speaks of the punishment that awaits those who dare to slander celestial beings (Jude 8-10). And yet, Christ is more awesome than all of the holy ones who surround him. In fact,

...when God brings his firstborn into the world, he says,

"Let *all* God's angels worship him." (Hebrews 1:6, emphasis mine)-

How awesome must our Christ be if he is so "superior to the angels" (Hebrews 1:4). He is more majestic than all who surround him put together.

IRRESISTIBLE CHRIST

More impressive to me than Matthew 25 is a word from Paul found in his second letter to the Thessalonians. Should we expect any resistance when Christ comes? Will evil, though doomed to fail, dare to put up a fight? Will even one angry, blaspheming word escape the lips of the evil one before he is utterly vanquished? This is what Paul has to say about the appearance of Christ:

And then the lawless one will be revealed, whom the Lord Jesus will overthrow with the breath of his mouth and destroy by the splendor of his coming. (2 Thessalonians 2:8)

His *breath* and his *splendor* are enough to vanquish evil. That's all. In a confrontation with unapproachable light, the darkness will vanish, as easily as turning on a light in a dark room. Even the mountains will melt like wax before him. As John vividly described, "Earth and sky fled from his presence, and there was no place for them" (Revelation 20:11).

On Judgment Day, we will be confronted by him who fills the universe. We will not just stand before God, but before *all* of God, as it were. There will be no place to run or hide because there will be nothing to run to. Poetic language aside, we will stand face to face with reality. Can you imagine Jesus being ashamed of us because we were ashamed of him? Even now, Christ fills the universe. He rules and reigns at the right hand of the Majesty in heaven, ready to return. He will come suddenly. James says that even now "the Judge is standing at the door" (James 5:9). And Peter says that he "is ready to judge" (1 Peter 4:5). Like a flash of lightning, the elements will burn up. Heaven and earth will be destroyed with a loud roar, and all mankind will "see him, even those who pierced him" (Revelation 1:7). They will mourn and cry for mountains to fall on them to hide them from the wrath of—the Lion? No, from "the wrath of the Lamb" (Revelation 6:16).

Jesus is a great king, yet he is gracious, kind and merciful. His greatness, his majesty, his royalty, was veiled while he was on the earth. He was born in a stable and surrounded by animals, not angels. He was an infant, vulnerable and helpless, nursing at a woman's breast.

> Sustainer of stars, nursing a breast,
> Creator of worlds, needing to rest,
> Word of God, unable to talk,
> Eternal in power, but can't even walk.
>
> H. K.

Jesus came first as a servant. He could be touched and handled. "He was crucified," Paul says, "in weakness" (2 Corinthians 13:4). There was "nothing in his appearance" to make us desire him, no "majesty to attract us to him" (Isaiah 53:2). When Jesus was arrested in the garden, it was with a kiss. The soldiers would not have known who he was, for there was no halo, no crown, no radiance. If they truly understood who he was, "they would not have crucified the Lord of glory" (1 Corinthians 2:8)—but they did. He was God, to be sure—the fullness of God—but he was also a man. His humanity hid the splendor of his divine glory. "He came to that which was his own, but his own did not receive him" (John 1:11).

But there was more to it than simply "not receiving him." Before his crucifixion, soldiers made a mockery of Jesus. They kicked him about like a rag doll. They hit him on the head again and again. They covered him with spit and placed a crown of thorns on his head. They placed a robe over his bleeding back and put a stick in his hand for a scepter. They fell down in mock worship before this Jesus, this King of the Jews, this enemy of Caesar, this idiot, this fool, this clown. However, that little production in a courtyard of pagans, that circle of cruel men, the mockery at the hands of ruthless thugs, was in fact the *coronation ceremony* of the King of the Universe! "I have installed my King on Zion, my holy hill" (Psalm 2:6). They did not know it—how could they have?

> A block of wood, a piece of meat—
> The butchers have their fun.
> Drawn and quartered, nice and neat—
> The slaughter has begun.
>
> H. K.

But at his Second Coming, there will be no mistaking his kingship. All mankind will mourn at his appearance!

SURPASSING SPLENDOR

When Christ was on the earth, his transcendent, even dangerous, splendor was hidden from the eyes of man. We could only see it in his words and deeds. He was approachable because the fullness of his glory was hidden. At a very touching moment during the Passover meal John, the beloved disciple, leaned on Jesus' breast, displaying the intimacy of their friendship. Though John had seen the transfiguration, the miracles, even the raising of the dead, he was not deterred from drawing near to his Lord. In his own words, "The life appeared; we have seen it" (1 John 1:2), "and our hands have touched" it (1 John 1:1). But when, near the close of his life, John was given a vision of Christ in his terrifying greatness, he "fell at his feet as though dead" (Revelation 1:17).

Our King, our Savior, our Lord is so awesome. We worship the Lamb and the Lion of God. He is the Lord of Love and the God of Glory. The way we understood Jesus to be on the earth is not necessarily how Jesus wants to be known now, in heaven, and it is certainly not how he will appear at his coming.

Consider the description of Jesus that is given in his revelation to John:

> His head and hair were white like wool, as white as snow, and his eyes were like blazing fire. His feet were like bronze glowing in a furnace, and his voice was like the sound of rushing waters. In his right hand he held seven stars, and out of his mouth came a sharp double-edged sword. His face was like the sun shining in all its brilliance.
>
> When I saw him, I fell at his feet as though dead. Then he placed his right hand on me and said: "Do not be afraid. I am the First and the Last. I am the Living One; I was dead, and behold I am alive for ever and ever! And I hold the keys of death and Hades." (Revelation 1:14-18)

Consider Jesus' descriptions of himself in his letters to the churches of Asia:

> "To the angel of the church in Ephesus write:
> These are the words of him who holds the seven stars in his right hand and walks among the seven golden lampstands." (Revelation 2:1)

> "To the angel of the church in Smyrna write:
> These are the words of him who is the First and the Last, who died and came to life again." (Revelation 2:8)

> "To the angel of the church in Pergamum write:
> These are the words of him who has the sharp, double-edged sword." (Revelation 2:12)

"To the angel of the church in Thyatira write:
These are the words of the Son of God, whose eyes are like blazing fire and whose feet are like burnished bronze." (Revelation 2:18)

"To the angel of the church in Sardis write:
These are the words of him who holds the seven spirits of God and the seven stars." (Revelation 3:1)

"To the angel of the church in Philadelphia write:
These are the words of him who is holy and true, who holds the key of David. What he opens no one can shut, and what he shuts no one can open." (Revelation 3:7)

"To the angel of the church in Laodicea write:
These are the words of the Amen, the faithful and true witness, the ruler of God's creation." (Revelation 3:14)

Consider the apocalyptic description of Jesus coming in judgment on the enemies of the church:

Then the kings of the earth, the princes, the generals, the rich, the mighty, and every slave and every free man hid in caves and among the rocks of the mountains. They called to the mountains and the rocks, "Fall on us and hide us from the face of him who sits on the throne and from the wrath of the Lamb! For the great day of their wrath has come, and who can stand?" (Revelation 6:15-17)

I saw heaven standing open and there before me was a white horse, whose rider is called Faithful and True. With justice he judges and makes war. His eyes are like blazing fire, and on his head are many crowns. He has a name written on him that no one knows but he himself. He is dressed in a robe dipped in blood, and his name is the Word of God. The armies of heaven were following him, riding on white horses and dressed in fine linen, white and clean. Out of his mouth comes a sharp sword with which to strike down the nations. "He will rule them

with an iron scepter." He treads the winepress of the fury of
the wrath of God Almighty. On his robe and on his thigh he
has this name written:

KING OF KINGS AND LORD OF LORDS.

(Revelation 19:11-16)

And consider the words of him who will return in judgment of all men:

"Behold, I am coming soon! My reward is with me, and I will
give to everyone according to what he has done. I am the
Alpha and the Omega, the First and the Last, the Beginning
and the End." (Revelation 22:12-13)

"I, Jesus, have sent my angel to give you this testimony for the
churches. I am the Root and the Offspring of David, and the
bright Morning Star." (Revelation 22:16)

He who testifies to these things says, "Yes, I am coming
soon."

Amen. Come, Lord Jesus.

The grace of the Lord Jesus be with God's people. Amen.
(Revelation 22:20-21)

This is the Christ of the Second Coming. How we stand before him
now, how we worship him now, how we approach him now will
determine how we will stand before him then. Let us see him as he is.
Let us bow low before the King. Let us fall down and kiss the Son.

Therefore God exalted him to the highest place
    and gave him the name that is above every name,
that at the name of Jesus every knee should bow,
    in heaven and on earth and under the earth,
and every tongue confess that Jesus Christ is Lord,
    to the glory of God the Father. (Philippians 2:9-11)

TRUE WORSHIPERS

The Father is looking for worshipers. So if you are looking for God and you just can't seem to find Him, then stop what you are doing and worship Him—and He will come and find you.

JOSEPH GARLINGTON

Worship is much more than an attitude toward God. Worship is our active service, our joyful and demanding work for God.

DONALD P. HUSTAD

Much Protestant worship has become flabby rather than holy, folksy rather than numinous, hortatory (exhorting) rather than adoring, and one is not surprised that it often appeals to infantile elements in human personality.

PAUL HUNE

Worship is telling the story of God's gracious, mighty acts on behalf of his people, and finding our place in the story.

KEN MEDEMA

Worship on Sunday "is meaningless unless it is proceeded by six days of worship as the way of life."

G. CAMPBELL MORGAN

Worship is an active response to God whereby we declare his work. Worship is not passive, but is participative. Worship is not simply a mood; it is a response. Worship is not just a feeling; it is a declaration.

RONALD ALLEN AND GORDON BORROR

10

Biplane Wonder

No one who is born of God will continue to sin, because God's seed remains in him; he cannot go on sinning, because he has been born of God.

1 John 3:9

I have great faith in a seed. Convince me a seed is there, and I am prepared for wonders.

H. D. Thoreau

The late, celebrated author Lewis Thomas was not usually given to the overuse of superlatives. However, when discussing the subject of embryology in his book, *The Medusa and the Snail*, he had this to say about the fertilized ovum, the solitary cell from which all human beings have come:

> The mere existence of that cell should be one of the great astonishments of the earth. People ought to be walking around all day, all through their waking hours, calling to each other in endless wonderment, talking of nothing except that cell.[1]

---

[1] Lewis R. Thomas, *The Medusa and the Snail* (New York: Viking Penguin, 1995), 156.

That little cell, barely visible to the naked eye, is shrouded in mystery. Who can explain how one single cell becomes hundreds of trillions of cells, perfectly placed, entirely integrated, *just so*? Furthermore, how does one kind of cell become hundreds of different kinds of cells—blood, bone, hair, lung, brain, heart, muscle, nerve, and more? Mr. Thomas concludes,

> If anyone does succeed in explaining it within my lifetime, I will charter a skywriting airplane, maybe a whole fleet of them, and send them aloft to write one great exclamation point after another, around the whole sky, until all my money runs out.[2]

START YOUR ENGINES!

Although I can, by faith, know the *reason* that cell is here, I can't explain how it happens; no one can. In fact, the professional lives of thousands of men and women, all of them brilliant, are centered around that single cell. For every question that is answered, ten more questions arise. Yet as wonderful as that human seed is—one of the great astonishments of life on earth—there is for the Christian another seed to be pondered, one that is outrageously more wonderful: God's own seed. This divine seed is deep within every born-again believer, within everyone who is "born of God" (1 John 3:9), implanted there by God himself.

The point of this chapter, to borrow from Henry David Thoreau, is to convince you that "a seed is there." And once convinced, to captivate your imagination. I approach this chapter with reverence and humility. I'm not trying to plunder the secret things of God—that would be folly, and I pray I'm not being presumptuous—that would be playing with fire. The concepts and ideas in this chapter are dear to my heart. They are not unique to me, however I have enjoyed thinking about them for the last fifteen years. Although I believe they are thoroughly Biblical, some may be unfamiliar, and they happen to be staggering in their implications. I would encourage you to fasten your seat belts, because what I am saying will leave you with only two choices—fall down and worship God or throw rocks at me!

---

[2] Thomas, 157.

Christ is the key to all that follows. He is the mystery made known, the deep secret revealed, "Christ in you, the hope of glory" (Colossians 1:27). Only God, from whom and to whom are all things, is to receive glory. Apart from Christ we are dust and ashes, nothing. Outside of Christ, we are "worthless" (Romans 3:12), "dead" (Ephesians 2:1), "by nature objects of [God's] wrath" (Ephesians 2:3). God in Christ, however, is the reason for everything. "To him be glory in the church and in Christ Jesus throughout all generations, for ever and ever! Amen" (Ephesians 3:21). This chapter is about God to be sure; but it is also about what God has done for us, his church. We represent one half, so to speak, of his eternal purpose.

Here is the heart of the matter. When the Bible calls us sons and daughters of God, it is *not* symbolic language. This is not some title given us merely to designate our allegiance to God the Father. It is not metaphor, hyperbole or allegory—it is a fact. We are children of God, "genetic" sons—the true spiritual offspring of God. "How great is the love the Father has lavished on us, that we should be called children of God!" writes John. And then, overwhelmed himself by wonder, and to make sure no one minimizes or doubts, he adds for emphasis, "And that is what we are!" (1 John 3:1). We are true spiritual sons and daughters, bona fide "heirs of God and co-heirs with Christ" (Romans 8:17), having the "full rights of sons" (Galatians 4:5).

God has imparted his very own life to us, the divine nature. We have been divinely regenerated, and truly adopted. We are "born again" (John 3:3), "born of the Spirit" (John 3:8), "born of God" (John 1:13), regenerated and renewed "by the Holy Spirit" (Titus 3:5). How? Because "the Spirit gives birth to spirit" (John 3:6). So radical is this new birth, we have become "new creation[s]" in Christ (2 Corinthians 5:17). "He chose us in him before the creation of the world...to be adopted as his sons" (Ephesians 1:4-5). Adopted into what? Born into what? The triune family of the eternal Godhead—Father, Son and Spirit. We are partakers of the divine nature without being divine. God's "genes," his "seed" (Greek: *sperma*) is inside us (1 John 3:9). We are truly, utterly, completely, genetically, 100% born of God!

Think about it: God's life is in me. What is more, his life is my life (see Colossians 3:1-4). We are regenerated from his divine life and have become, I say this reverently, a kind of extension of the original cosmic family. This is Biblical revelation and should be accepted as truth. As we digest and ponder and *accept* it—we will glory in it. Grasping this truth should increase our confidence in Christ a thousandfold. Our identity in Christ, the fact that we are true sons and daughters of God, should be the supreme delight of our souls.

BROUGHT TO GLORY

God's purpose for humankind, his eternal purpose, is clear: the creation of a new humanity, a brand new race, through the glorification of his children.

> In bringing many sons to glory, it was fitting that God, for whom and through whom everything exists, should make the author of their salvation perfect through suffering. Both the one who makes men holy and those who are made holy are of the same family. So Jesus is not ashamed to call them brothers. (Hebrews 2:10-11)

> For those God foreknew he also predestined to be conformed to the likeness of his Son, that he might be the firstborn among many brothers. And those he predestined, he also called; those he called, he also justified; those he justified, he also glorified. (Romans 8:29-30)

Christ is the "firstborn among many brothers." This is the miracle of redemption. God not only created us, but also recreated us, imparting his own life to us through the process of new birth. Christ is the prototype and the pattern; he is the power, the purpose and ultimately the praise of our redemption. Christ, "the image of the invisible God" (Colossians 1:15), assumed and inhabited the nature of man, but only because man has been made in *his image*—he is forever "the man Christ Jesus" (1 Timothy 2:5). We are created in God's image, after his likeness.

Through the incarnation and the cross, the Son of God not only shared our humanity (Hebrews 2:14), taking our flesh and blood, but he also bore our sin (Isaiah 53:5). Somehow, by this mysterious exchange of natures, he has imparted to *us* the holiness and glory and righteousness of God in return.

> God made him who had no sin to be sin for us, so that in him we might become the righteousness of God. (2 Corinthians 5:21)

> It is because of him that you are in Christ Jesus, who has become for us wisdom from God—that is, our righteousness, holiness and redemption. (1 Corinthians 1:30)

> God has chosen to make known…the glorious riches of this mystery, which is Christ in you, the hope of glory. (Colossians 1:27)

You may think I am propagating the deification of man. I am not, no way, never—that would be heresy. Man is never deified, but he *is* glorified. And I believe this exaltation and glorification of man is a billionfold richer than we could ever hope to realize in this lifetime. How could one cell at conception imagine itself becoming hundreds of trillions of times greater? In the same way, can we ever fully imagine what will become of us in glory? We must wake up to the wonders of just who we are in Christ!

As children of God, we enjoy enormous benefits from our privileged relationship, our cosmic status.

> But when the time had fully come, God sent his Son, born of a woman, born under law, to redeem those under law, that we might receive the full rights of sons. Because you are sons, God sent the Spirit of his Son into our hearts, the Spirit who calls out, "*Abba,* Father." So you are no longer a slave, but a son; and since you are a son, God has made you also an heir. (Galatians 4:4-7)

What kind of rights? "Full rights." Heirs of whom? Of God. What do we own? "The whole estate"! (See Galatians 4:1.)

My own children, Daniel and Natassja, are both adopted. Marilyn and I love them completely—truly, madly and deeply. I cannot love them more than I do. They are mine—my family, my son and daughter. Although adopted, they have my name and are my legal heirs. They are co-heirs, judicial equals. Yet our adoption into God's family is far richer, more real, way deeper than even this. He has not simply given us life, but his divine life,

> ...through the washing of rebirth and renewal by the Holy Spirit, whom he poured out on us generously through Jesus Christ our Savior, so that, having been justified by his grace, we might become heirs having the hope of eternal life. (Titus 3:5-7)

CROWNING ACHIEVEMENT

Apart from God himself, redeemed humanity is the highest order of created being in the universe, visible or invisible. I'm not talking about carnal man, fallen and sinful; but regenerate, redeemed, glorified man. In Christ—and *that* is the secret—we are greater even than the angels, outranking them in authority and splendor. Angels are, of course, unimaginably splendorous, intelligent and powerful; I am in no way diminishing their magnificence. However, even though they stand in the presence of God, even though they see his face, angels will always be under us, in submission to us, because we are the sons and daughters of God.

> Are not all angels ministering spirits sent to serve those who will inherit salvation? (Hebrews 1:14)

Angels are not God's sons in the way we are. They are created, but we are recreated. Angels are not created in the image of God as we are. Jesus did not die for angels, but for us who are created in the image of God. It would seem that angels cannot be redeemed or regenerated by God's life when they sin; we are not told of any plan of salvation for them (see 2 Peter 2:4).

Angels are magnificent beings, and yet,

> ...to which of the angels did God ever say,
>
>> "You are my Son;
>>   today I have become your Father"?
>
> Or again,
>
>> "I will be his Father,
>>   and he will be my Son"? (Hebrews 1:5)

Only to Jesus Christ, preeminent in glory, and to us, his brothers and children, did God ever say such a thing. Christ is "the One and Only, who came from the Father, full of grace and truth" (John 1:14). He is eternally preeminent. However, we are also his children (Hebrews 2:13), his brothers (Romans 8:29), "of the same family" (Hebrews 2:11). We too are God's sons. The proof of this comes from God himself:

> Because you are sons, God sent the Spirit of his Son into our hearts, the Spirit who calls out, "*Abba,* Father." (Galatians 4:6)

This is never spoken to angels.

I am cautious on this point, not wishing to minimize the glory and power and intelligence of these celestial beings, or their privileged status before God. To the contrary, to behold an angel is to be suddenly terrorized. I love the powerful imagery of this poem.

> Every angel is terrifying. But if the archangel now, perilous,
>   from behind the stars
> took even one step down toward us: our own heart, beating
> higher and higher, would beat us to death. Who are you?
> Early successes, creation's pampered favorites,
> Mountain ranges, peaks growing red in the dawn
> Of all beginning, pollen of the flowering Godhead,
> Joints of pure light, corridors, stairways, thrones,
> Space formed from essence, shields made of ecstasy,
> Storms of emotion whirled into rapture, and suddenly,
>   alone;

> *Mirrors* would scoop up the beauty that has streamed from
>> their face
> And gather it back, into themselves, entire.[4]
>> Rainer Maria Rilke

Angels are awesome to be sure, but spiritually we outrank them; they are our servants. And if you can accept it, the least in the kingdom of God is greater in rank than even the archangel Michael. In the age to come, we shall reign with Christ over the entire universe, including angels. To the Corinthians, Paul says matter-of-factly and to their shame,

> Do you not know that the saints will judge the world?...Do you not know that we will judge angels? (1 Corinthians 6:2-3)

Let this soak in. We—the church—are the longing of angels. (See 1 Peter 1:12.) Of course, there will always be an infinite distinction between God and us. Through Christ, however, we are as close to God and as much *like God* as a created being can be without violating or breaching the Godhead itself. This is the glory of who we are in Christ. This is the reality and mystery of our union with Christ.

Bone of His Bone

We are true sons of God right now. Although we eagerly await our full adoption as sons, our union, our oneness with Christ, is completely real right now.

> "On that day you will realize that I am in my Father, and you are in me, and I am in you." (John 14:20)

We are in Christ and Christ is in us. We are in Christ and he is in God. We are "of Christ, and Christ is of God" (1 Corinthians 3:23). We simply cannot be nearer or closer to God than we are right now. The Day will come when we will finally "realize" this. In the meantime, though the fullness of our glory will not be fully realized until the last day, it is nonetheless very real *right now.*

---

[4] Stephen Maria Rilke and Stephen Mitchell (translator), "The Second Elegy," *The Selected Poetry of Rainer Maria Rilke* (New York: Vintage Books, 1989).

So nigh, so very nigh to God, I cannot nearer be;
For in the Person of His Son, I am as near as He.

REES HOWELLS

Christ is our life. We are so intimately and inextricably bound to him that his destiny becomes our destiny.

> When Christ, who is your life, appears, then you also will appear with him in glory. (Colossians 3:4)

God's Spirit dwells in us. His Holy Spirit is inside each and every one of us who belong to him right now. Ponder the majesty of this truth. The "Holy, Holy, Holy" Spirit of God lives inside of you and me. What majesty! What mystery! What glory! How could this be unless we were true sons and truly forgiven?

> Do you not know that your body is a temple of the Holy Spirit, who is in you, whom you have received from God? (1 Corinthians 6:19)

> Don't you know that you yourselves are God's temple and that God's Spirit lives in you? ...for God's temple is sacred, and you are that temple. (1 Corinthians 3:16-17)

> For in Christ all the fullness of the Deity lives in bodily form, and you have been given fullness in Christ, who is the head over every power and authority. (Colossians 2:9-10)

When Adam and Eve were joined together, God said, "They will become one flesh" (Genesis 2:24). Quoting this text, Paul says "This is a profound mystery—but I am talking about Christ and the church" (Ephesians 5:32). We are the bride of Christ, the "wife of the Lamb" (Revelation 21:9), his co-heir and co-sovereign. We are his Eve, and he is our Adam. Now if our husband is the king of the universe, then who are we? Nothing less than his queen and counterpart in paradise.

For what reason does Paul urge the Corinthians to repent of their sexual immorality?

> Do you not know that your bodies are members of Christ himself? Shall I then take the members of Christ and unite them with a prostitute? Never! Do you not know that he who unites himself with a prostitute is one with her in body? For it is said, "The two will become one flesh." But he who unites himself with the Lord *is one with him in spirit.* (1 Corinthians 6:15-17, emphasis mine)

Our oneness with Christ is a living, vital, organic unity; not by mingling or mixing, but as bone of his bone and flesh of his flesh. Even now, in Christ, we are seated with him in the heavenly realms (Ephesians 2:4-7). Even now "we have confidence to enter the Most Holy Place" (Hebrews 10:19). We are "in Christ" (Romans 8:1), "clothed...with Christ" (Galatians 3:27), "united with [Christ]" (Romans 6:5). Christ is in all and through all.

In Christ, we "participate in the divine nature" (2 Peter 1:4). We share the invincible life of God. In Christ, we are as holy, as righteous, as God himself (2 Corinthians 5:21), able to stand before him "confident and unashamed" (1 John 2:28). We are the dwelling of his Holy Spirit, fully united with him—"one with him in spirit" (1 Corinthians 6:17).

BECAUSE YOU ARE SONS

We are God's treasured possession, a people who are his very own.

> He has declared that he will set you in praise, fame and honor high above all the nations he has made and that you will be a people holy to the LORD your God, as he promised. (Deuteronomy 26:19)

We are the joy of every generation, "on whom the fulfillment of the ages has come" (1 Corinthians 10:11). We are the apple of his eye, carved on the palm of his hand, chosen before creation, chosen by grace, enveloped by his fierce and awesome love, "predestined to be conformed to the likeness of his Son" (Romans 8:29)—"the Son he loves" (Colossians 1:13).

Know this for sure: God loves us as much as he loves Christ himself, and Christ loves us as much as the Father loves him (John 17:23, 15:9). God "did not spare his own Son, but gave him up for us all" (Romans 8:32). And because of this extravagant lavishing of divine love, the original cosmic family—Father, Son and Spirit—has become a larger, more extended circle of fellowship.

> Both the one who makes men holy and those who are made holy are of the same family. So Jesus is not ashamed to call them brothers. (Hebrews 2:11)

As Jesus prayed,

> "you...have loved them even as you have loved me.
> "Father, I want those you have given me to be with me where I am, and to see my glory, the glory you have given me because you loved me before the creation of the world.
> "...in order that the love you have for me may be in them and that I myself may be in them." (John 17:23-24,26)

Why? How? What are the implications of all this?

NOTHING HELD BACK

There is simply no more God can do for us. He has given us "all things" (Romans 8:32), "every spiritual blessing" (Ephesians 1:3). There is no more love to be given—all is lavished on us right now. There is no more glory that can be given or shared—we have his glory. We cannot be exalted to a higher position than we are right now—seated with Christ in the heavenly realms (Ephesians 2:6).

Consider these amazing passages, and try to fathom the unfathomable!

> All things are yours, whether Paul or Apollos or Cephas or the world or life or death or the present or the future—all are yours, and you are of Christ, and Christ is of God. (1 Corinthians 3:21-23)

"...for your Father has been pleased to give you the kingdom." (Luke 12:32)

"I will give [you] authority over the nations...just as I have received authority from my Father." (Revelation 2:26-27)

"...you will be with me in paradise." (Luke 23:43)

"...in the paradise of God." (Revelation 2:7)

"I have given them the glory that you gave me...." (John 17:22)

...heirs of God and co-heirs with Christ... (Romans 8:17)

"Come and share your master's happiness!" (Matthew 25:21)

"...my peace..." (John 14:27)

"...my joy..." (John 15:11)

...so that in him we might become the righteousness of God. (2 Corinthians 5:21)

Christ...is your life.... (Colossians 3:4)

God...calls you into his kingdom and glory. (1 Thessalonians 2:12)

...into the kingdom of the Son he loves... (Colossians 1:13)

...every spiritual blessing... (Ephesians 1:3)

But we have the mind of Christ. (1 Corinthians 2:16)

You have been given fullness in Christ. (Colossians 2:10)

...the church, which is his body, the fullness of him who fills everything in every way. (Ephesians 1:22-23)

The saints will judge the world. (1 Corinthians 6:2)

We will judge angels. (1 Corinthians 6:3)

...full rights of sons. (Galatians 4:5)

[We own] the whole estate. (Galatians 4:1)

...incomparable riches... (Ephesians 2:7)

…unsearchable riches… (Ephesians 3:8)

…indescribable gift! (2 Corinthians 9:15)

…immeasurably more… (Ephesians 3:20)

…inexpressible things… (2 Corinthians 12:4)

…the full riches of complete understanding…all the treasures of wisdom and knowledge. (Colossians 2:2-3)

Can we be sure? Are we dreaming? Deluded? Is this a flight of fancy or megalomania? Not at all!

He who did not spare his own Son, but gave him up for us all—how will he not also, along with him, graciously give us all things?

…For I am convinced that neither death nor life, neither angels nor demons, neither the present nor the future, nor any powers, neither height nor depth, nor anything else in all creation, will be able to separate us from the love of God that is in Christ Jesus our Lord. (Romans 8:32, 38-39)

Indeed, the entire cosmos serves the needs of God's children.

We know that in all things God works for the good of those who love him, who have been called according to his purpose. (Romans 8:28)

We share a partnership with Christ that is real and consequential. We are heirs of God and co-heirs with Christ—wrap your mind around that one! And like the first Adam and Eve, who were to have dominion over the earth, we too shall exercise dominion and authority "over the nations" (Revelation 2:26) with our Lord and Savior as we rule the next universe with him.

"To him who overcomes, I will give the right to sit with me on my throne, just as I overcame and sat down with my Father on his throne." (Revelation 3:21)

We share his glory, his kingdom, his throne, his life, his spirit, his reign, his seed, his power, his likeness, his fullness and his joy. We are exalted to the nth degree, glorified to the fullest possible extent, empowered to become as much like Christ as human beings can become.

> But our citizenship is in heaven. And we eagerly await a Savior from there, the Lord Jesus Christ, who, by the power that enables him to bring everything under his control, will transform our lowly bodies so that they will be like his glorious body. (Philippians 3:20-21)

> The first man was of the dust of the earth, the second man from heaven. As was the earthly man, so are those who are of the earth; and as is the man from heaven, so also are those who are of heaven. And just as we have borne the likeness of the earthly man, so shall we bear the likeness of the man from heaven. (1 Corinthians 15:47-49)

> Dear friends, now we are children of God, and what we will be has not yet been made known. But we know that when he appears, we shall be like him, for we shall see him as he is. (1 John 3:2)

And now, as a church, we are "a kind of firstfruits of all he created" (James 1:18). To God alone be the glory. To God alone be eternal praise.

> For from him and through him and to him are all things.
> To him be the glory forever! Amen. (Romans 11:36)

PINNACLE OF CREATION

What is the purpose of this universe, this vast cosmos? It is we—the elect of God. Secular scientists, with all their particle accelerators, picks and shovels, gizmos and Geiger-counters, telescopes and microscopes, have no idea. Modern cosmologists "believe the whole universe started from a point (a singularity) thousands of times smaller than a pinhead"[5]—a quantum fluctuation in a sea of potential energy. Furthermore, it is widely held that one day the whole cosmos will be defined

---

[5] Leon Lederman with Dick Teresi, *The God Particle* (New York: Dell Publishing Company, Inc., 1993), 387.

and explained mathematically by a Grand Unified Theory—by a simple equation. In his book *The God Particle,* physicist Leon Lederman states it like this: "My ambition is to live to see all of physics reduced to a formula so elegant and simple that it will easily fit on the front of a T-shirt"[6]—as if an equation had power to bring things to life! Most believe that we are here "by an extremely fortuitous accident" and that mankind is therefore insignificant, "lost in the immensity of the cosmos."[7] Bertrand Russell nicely summarizes this philosophy of despair.

> That man is the product of causes which had no prevision of the end they were achieving; that his origin, his growth, his hopes and fears, his loves and his beliefs, are but the outcome of accidental collocations of atoms; that no fire, no heroism, no intensity of thought and feeling, can preserve an individual life beyond the grave; that all the labor of the ages, all the devotion, all the inspirations, all the noonday brightness of human genius, are destined to extinction in the vast depth of the solar system, and that the whole temple of Man's achievement must inevitably be buried beneath the debris of a universe in ruins—all these things, if not quite beyond dispute, are yet so nearly certain, that no philosophy which rejects them can hope to stand. Only within the scaffolding of these truths, only on the firm foundation of unyielding despair, can the soul's habitation henceforth be safely built. Brief and powerless is man's life, on him and all his race the slow, sure doom falls pitiless and dark.[8]

Ouch! Buy the man a flower. Consider the similar view espoused by Carl Sagan.

> "There is nothing special about us," declares Carl Sagan. "We are not at the center of the solar system; our planet is

---

[6] Lederman with Teresi, 21.

[7] John D. Barrow and Frank J. Tipler, *The Anthropic Cosmological Principle* (Oxford, NY: Oxford Univ. Press, 1988), 613.

[8] Bertrand Russell, *Why I Am Not a Christian and Other Essays* (New York: Simon and Schuster, 1976), 107.

one of many... the sun is just another star, obscurely located,
one among some 400 billion others in the Milky Way, which
in turn is one galaxy among perhaps hundreds of billions....
We do not posses any uniquely valid locale, epoch, velocity,
acceleration, or means of measuring space and time."[9]

In a nutshell, we are not special or unique at all. We are a cosmic
accident in a meaningless universe. And yet, here we are—looking up,
pondering, building civilizations and hospitals and Taj Mahals. What is
so ordinary about that?

Other scientists seem to be a bit more circumspect.

As we look out into the universe and identify the many
accidents of physics and astronomy that have worked together to our benefit, it almost seems as if the universe must
in some sense have known that we were coming.[10]

Concerning the fine tuning of our universe, Sir Fred Hoyle, the
Nobel prizewinning physicist, has this to say:

A common sense interpretation of the facts suggests that a
super-intellect has monkeyed with Physics, as well as with
Chemistry and Biology, and that there are no blind forces
worth speaking about in nature. The numbers one calcu-
lates from the facts seem to me so overwhelming as to put
this conclusion almost beyond question.[11]

Even Stephen Hawking admits there must be more, and wonders
aloud:

Even if there is only one possible unified theory, it is just a set
of rules and equations. What is it that breathes *fire* into the
equations and makes a universe for them to describe?
...Why is it that we and the universe exist? If we find the

---

[9] Carl Sagan and W. I. Newman, *Quarterly J. R. Astron.*, soc. 24, 113 (1983).
[10] Barrow and Tipler, 318.
[11] Timothy Ferris, *The Whole Shebang* (New York: Simon and Schuster, 1997), 305.

answer to that, it would be the ultimate triumph of human reason—for then we would know the mind of God."[12]

Secular scientists don't have a clue as to why we exist. Philosophers can only pretend to understand the meaning of the universe and why we are here, but they too are hollow windbags, philosophical stickmen. Humanistic historians can only guess. And yet, some poor peasant in Bangladesh, a Christian working in his field with a tattered New Testament in his pocket, is able to comprehend God's one eternal purpose in this universe—himself, and the church of Christ. Why is that? Because he has the mind of God! (See 1 Corinthians 2:9-16.) I love that our brothers and sisters in Bangladesh possess the unsearchable riches of God. I love that our brothers and sisters in Africa are the radiant bride of Christ. I love that all the saints in India, especially the weakest and "most despised" among them, shall be exalted with Christ on his throne in heavenly glory. I love that our brothers and sisters in South America shall eat fruit from the tree of life and feast in the paradise of God. And I love that our brothers and sisters in China will one day share in the redemption and freedom of this whole universe.

Indeed, the universe itself is on tiptoes, holding its breath and groaning, eagerly awaiting that final hour when God's children are freed. And only then, with redeemed humanity, will the universe itself experience redemption (Romans 8:18-23).

The church is so central, and so bound to this cosmos, and this universe, this heaven and earth so inextricably bound to us—that our fate becomes its fate. When man sinned, the *entire cosmos* was affected. But it is only through our glorification and freedom as redeemed sons of God that the universe itself will be brought into our redemption and liberation—not ahead of us, not behind us, but with us. Creation is good, but redemption is better by far. How does one explain this to an unregenerate mind? How can one ever begin to comprehend this outside of Christ? He can't. "But we have the mind of Christ" (1 Corinthians 2:16).

---

[12] Stephen Hawking, *A Brief History of Time* (New York: Bantam Books, Inc., 1998), 191.

Twenty-first century man considers it the height of arrogance for us to assume that we are alone in this universe, let alone the reason for it. Or, as Carl Sagan said via Jodie Foster's character in the movie *Contact*, "It would seem like an awful waste of space." I believe, however, this entire universe, billions of light years across, seemingly infinite in all directions, with countless orbs and stars, every nation, all of history, every angel, visible and invisible things, *every* thing, *all* things were created, ultimately, for us—the few, the elect of God, those chosen in Christ before the creation of the world. This whole cosmos came into being not simply for the sake of humanity, but ultimately and especially, for redeemed humanity.

"In the beginning God created the heavens and the earth" (Genesis 1:1). From the first verse of Scripture, our place is unique, special, chosen. The earth is God's stage. We are the visited planet. God is accomplishing his eternal drama right here and right now, on this planet, for us. Christ was born once, incarnated. Christ has died once, for our sins. On this planet, and no other, has God said, "I have installed my King on Zion" (Psalm 2:6).

The purpose of the heavens and the earth is for bringing many sons to glory. Of course, the immensity of this universe, and the magnitude of God's purposes and plans, utterly humble us. On the other hand, at the same time, we should feel privileged, special, incredibly awed to think that it is all for us, the church, the bride of Christ.

GLORY IN THE CHURCH

Why did God make everything in the first place? He didn't need anything at all. In and of himself he is complete and perfect and glorious. God did this to court us, to woo us, to awaken us so that his elect, his chosen by grace, would reach out and find him. The blessings of courtship, marriage, children, family and love are not only the most important aspects of humanity, but also a *type* or foreshadowing of God's higher purpose in creation. Romance and love is the heart and soul of the cosmos. All of it—the whole shebang, the entire reason for its existence—is for the selection and preparation of a bride for Christ, an eternal companion.

Paul told the Corinthians that all things, whether life or death, are for us. In Ephesians, Christ rules the universe—for us. In Colossians, all things visible or invisible, whether thrones or powers or rulers or authorities were made for him, the image of the invisible God and the firstborn over all creation, but it is we, the church, who are the focus and recipients of this cosmic adventure. Every act of God, every faraway and flaming galaxy, every king, every priest, every nation, every molecule and mite, every wind and wave, every animal and insect, every last atom, came into being for the sake of the church, "his body, the fullness of him who fills everything in every way" (Ephesians 1:23). History moves forward on our behalf. Earthly kingdoms rise and fall on our behalf, to serve us, the kingdom of God, and to accomplish God's purposes for his chosen race. (See Romans 13:1-7.)

I'm not saying that we are the geographical center of the universe. But that should not cause us to doubt the favored status of our planet, the human race or the church. Jesus was born in Bethlehem, not Jerusalem. He died outside of the city, not on the temple mount. Furthermore, the immensity of this universe, the mind-numbing vastness of space, should not be the cause of doubt or disbelief. We *are* puny in the physical scheme of things. But so what? Our smallness has nothing to do with our significance. After all, the infinite God reduced himself to the size of an ovum in the womb of a teenage virgin. Let us fall down and worship and praise our God forever for "the incomparable riches of his grace, expressed in his kindness to us in Christ Jesus" (Ephesians 2:7).

Christ—the Lamb that was slain before the world began (Revelation 13:8)—was given as a sacrifice for and Savior of the world, but "especially of those who believe" (1 Timothy 4:10). We were called and chosen before creation to be in Christ Jesus, "holy and blameless in his sight" (Ephesians 1:4). The whole of creation exists for the accomplishment of God's one eternal purpose. And we, the church, the elect of God, the *few*—called, chosen and faithful—are the beneficiaries of that purpose. We can assume, therefore, with profound wonder and humility, that the sole reason for the universe—this unimaginably vast plenum of galaxies and living things; and the whole history of mankind—the rise and fall of nations, every civilization, the establishment of all governments and kings, communist or capitalist; as well as everything that has ever existed—angels and demons, life and suffering, birth and death, marriage and family, the Jews, the temple, the Law and the Prophets; every law of nature—gravity and light and thermodynamics, the motion of the heavenly spheres, trees and flowers, sun and moon, solar systems and solar eclipses, oceans and atmospheres, quasars, neutron stars and black holes, thunder and lightning, and the air we breathe; every last man or woman, good or bad—all are for us, for the purpose of "bringing many sons to glory" (Hebrews 2:10).

To the unredeemed, man might as well be an accident, life is meaningless, and we are only a few genes different from a monkey. Our ancestors came from Darwin's "warm little pond." We are the products of chance, as if chance had some divine power! To the skeptic, we are insignificant, and it is the epitome of arrogance to even suggest that we have some sort of special place in this hostile universe, let alone a divinely conceived one. In this scenario, it is the Christian outlook that is arrogant, suffocating and irrational. To the unbeliever, we were born in a fiery Bang, and we will die in a cold and pointless and pitiless universe. And that is all.

We, on the other hand, know that

> ...he chose us in him before the creation of the world. (Ephesians 1:4)

and that

> ...in all things God works for the good of those who love him, who have been called according to his purpose. (Romans 8:28)

In addition,

> "All things are yours, whether Paul or Apollos or Cephas or the world or life or death or the present or the future—all are

yours, and you are of Christ, and Christ is of God."
(1 Corinthians 3:21-23)

All things means all things, visible and invisible, in this whole created universe. God is orchestrating "all things" for the purpose of bringing many sons to glory, and for the good of those who love him, who have been called according to his purpose. As Christians, we are the reason for the universe. God wanted to bring many sons to glory and the physical cosmos is the setting for this divine drama. It is the stage, the arena, the battleground, the vale of soul making. Only once has God incarnated and died—and it was on our earth, for us.

Does this humble us? Of course it does. But at the same time, rather than feeling lost and insignificant amidst the immensity of the countless starry host in space, we as a church should be overwhelmed with awe and gratitude by the special place we have in the universe. This cosmos, made to be a home and suitable habitation for us, is a cathedral of wonder. It is here that God makes his invisible nature plain to see. It is for signs and seasons and for bringing about good things for the benefit of man. The universe declares the power and glory of God.

Declares it to whom? To us. And why? For us. Every flower is a cathedral, every star an oracle. Every shell, every rainbow, every seed is a herald, a preacher and a trumpet calling us Godward. In a sense, the universe is a woman. She is a womb, a *midwife* giving birth to sons of God. (See Romans 8:16-30.)

THE VISITED PLANET

It was here, on this visited planet, that "God sent his Son, born of a woman, born under law, to redeem those under law, that we might receive the full rights of sons" (Galatians 4:4-5). And it is here, on our little planet—a fragile, silky, little droplet in the deep blackness of space—that the stage is set for God's eternal drama. On this tiny speck of dust, in the village of Bethlehem, in the womb of a virgin, the eternal, infinite Son of God was conceived. And on our earth, outside the walls of Jerusalem, on a hill of dirt, he was crucified, he bled and he died. All of this was for us, the elect of God, that we might become a "suitable helper" (Genesis 2:20) for Jesus, created from his side, his blood, his bone. Romance is the reason for everything. Romance is the explanation for Thomas' cell.

I wish Lewis Thomas were still alive. Perhaps these scriptures and ideas would have stirred him to deeper questioning, even to a relationship with God. The seed he wrote about, rhapsodized about, is the seed of man created in the image of God, after his likeness. It is a remarkable and glorious seed, albeit of flesh and blood. What is to become of the greater seed, the divine seed, planted deep within every disciple of Christ—the seed of God? Prepare for wonders. Exponential wonders. Skywriting wonders. Biplane wonders.

11

ELEMENTAL THINGS

T he carbon atom is almost magical. With just a twist of its atomic structure, pure carbon can become either a diamond or a chunk of coal. One is black, the other is clear and colorless. One is soft and one is hard. One absorbs light, while the other reflects and refracts light. One is for the barbecue; the other is for a bride to be.

When we look around at the countless millions of material things in our universe, it is hard to believe that everything that exists is formed out of only 106 elements—such as hydrogen, oxygen, nitrogen, sodium and carbon. And amazingly, every quality of matter—the smell, texture, taste, color, softness, hardness, slipperiness, shininess, weight, viscosity, brittleness, malleability, translucence or opacity—is based on how these few elements interact.

Or consider music. Millions of tunes exist, from symphonies to jigs, from raps to polkas. Yet all of the nuances of composition that reflect the variety of human cultures—whether Indonesian, Indian, South American or Chinese—all are played with the same basic set of notes.

Or take higher learning. No matter how sophisticated the subject matter, everything is based upon what was learned in an elementary education: the grasping of ABCs and 123s.

What amazing things are produced by a few chemical elements, a few basic notes or a few letters: symphonies that are either glorious or dull; chemicals that make coal or diamonds, poison or food; words that hurt or heal, delight or terrify.

What follows are the chemicals and notes, the basic elements that comprise true worship. These are the essentials, the ABCs, of worship.

How we incorporate each one, to what degree and in what proportion, for how long and with what intensity will determine the nature of our composition. To worship God, we must become intimately familiar with these fundamental elements.

Spirit and Truth

Everything about Jesus was wonderful and surprising. When he chose to reveal himself for the first time as Messiah, it was not to a man, but to a woman; not to a Jew, but to a Samaritan; not to a priest, but to a profligate, whose life was all but shattered by sin (John 4:1-42). He was kind—a gentleman even—disarming her by asking a favor. And then, to her surprise, he put her cup to his lips. What Jew would have done that? What Rabbi would have even been in Samaria, let alone have said one word to her?

When the subject of worship came up, Jesus wiped out seven hundred years of tradition, ritual and sacrifice with just one sentence: "You...worship what you do not know," and that was that (John 4:22). He was kind, but not sentimental. Truth is crucial to God, and he is serious about the hows and whys of worship. In fact, it is not just worship that God seeks, but *truth* in worship. God wants true worshipers—men and women who will devote themselves to him, who love him and long for him.

> "Yet a time is coming and has now come when the true worshipers will worship the Father in spirit and truth, for they are the kind of worshipers the Father seeks. God is spirit, and his worshipers must worship in spirit and in truth." (John 4:23-24)

Jesus changed everything. That was his divine prerogative, of course—one greater than the Sabbath was here, one greater than Solomon was here, one greater than the temple was here. Worship was no longer to be about a place, but a person, a presence. To be sure, Jerusalem and the temple were not planned by men but by God. Nevertheless, Christ would change all that. We are no longer bound by geography, sacred buildings, animal sacrifice or any physical thing at all—we need only a bit of space and time, bread and wine. We are now free to worship God anywhere and any time we want—inside or out, in jail, by a river, on the beach or in a building if we choose.

Why is that? Because *we* are his temple now. His glory fills each and every one of us who are the church, "the fullness of him who fills everything in every way" (Ephesians 1:23). We are the dwelling of his Holy Spirit, each a living stone, each a temple in our own right, placed within a greater temple, a building not made with hands, one that "rises to become a holy temple in the Lord...a dwelling in which God lives by his Spirit" (Ephesians 2:21-22). And even this temple, the church, lies within the greater temple in heaven itself, before the altar and throne of God. Imagine—a temple within a temple within a temple, like those Russian dolls we enjoy taking apart.

Even though we are not bound by physical limitations, Jesus reveals two essentials that are binding for us. Acceptable worship must proceed in Spirit and in truth. What does it mean to worship *in Spirit?* I believe this means heartfelt, inward and sincere worship of God. Such worship has its source in love that flows from a river deep within (John 7:38). We worship God emotionally, in the joy of his Spirit, as Christ himself did. We "see" him with the eyes of our hearts (Ephesians 1:18). We "pray in the Spirit" (Ephesians 6:18), "worship by the Spirit" (Philippians 3:3), and sing "spiritual songs" (Colossians 3:16). "Deep calls to deep" (Psalm 42:7) and Spirit communes with spirit. The mortal and inward touches the immortal and invisible.

Because worship is prayer, the Spirit also helps us. He

> ...intercedes for us with groans that words cannot express. And he who searches our hearts knows the mind of the Spirit, because the Spirit intercedes for the saints in accordance with God's will. (Romans 8:26-27)

We no longer offer blood sacrifices, but a dual sacrifice of praise—"the fruit of lips that confess his name" (Hebrews 13:15) and of our lives, offered daily to him—our "spiritual act of worship" (Romans 12:1). "In Spirit" means that we approach God with a pure heart and holy hands, with a clear conscience and with integrity. We should be expressive, overflowing with thanksgiving and gratitude.

Perhaps more than anyone else, David exemplified the spiritual heart that Jesus desires. He praised God deeply, honestly, emotionally and consistently—throughout the peaks and valleys of his life. He gave sacrificially, and his love for God was evident to all. He was humbled by his own sinfulness and let himself be broken and molded by God. He expressed the true thoughts of his heart and delighted in the evidence of God all around him. His many psalms give us a full range of emotions, from love, praise and adoration to depression, anxiety and fear. His honesty and realness before God shock us at times. We see a man wrestling with his own unworthiness, but at the same time, striving to grasp the awesomeness and mystery of God. As "a man after [God's] own heart" (1 Samuel 13:14), David is worthy of our respect and imitation.

What, then, is worshiping *in truth?* Worshiping in truth engages our minds as well as our hearts. We are commanded to love God with all of our minds and to grow in our knowledge of him. We must think Biblically about the nature and ways of God, purging from our minds the idolatrous concepts that hurt and impair our worship. Idolatry is not just bowing down to golden calves; it also means having a "puny" God that we hold in our imagination. In his book *The Knowledge of the Holy*, A. W. Tozer correctly surmises that a right conception of God is to worship what the foundation is to the temple. "Where it is inadequate or out of plumb the whole structure must sooner or later collapse. ...The heaviest obligation lying upon the Christian church today is to purify and elevate her concept of God until it is once more worthy of him—and of her."[1]

We cannot truly worship an almighty God who is not absolutely sovereign. We cannot be thankful and intimate with God if we doubt his love. We cannot entrust ourselves to a God who is not omnipotent, who has lost even one battle to the evil one, or who can do wrong—even once. We cannot truly worship God if we believe events are out of his

[1] A. W. Tozer, *The Knowledge of the Holy* (New York: HarperCollins Publishers, Inc., 1975), 4.

control or if we suspect he needs to read a newspaper to find out what's going on in the world! We won't revere God if we doubt that he created this universe with perfect design and intent or doubt if he is pervasively involved in his creation.

Just as we will not rise above our concept of God in our everyday lives, we cannot rise above our concept of God in our worship. Jesus prayed:

> "Now this is eternal life: that they may *know* you, the only true God, and Jesus Christ, whom you have sent." (John 17:3, emphasis mine)

An infantile concept of God will profoundly impair our ability to offer true worship, not to mention jeopardize our entire spiritual life.

Worship in truth therefore involves a deep commitment to God's word. God has exalted above all things his name and his word (Psalm 119). The Scriptures are so bound to the divine nature that the psalmist could praise God's law without guilt of "bibliolatry." Mature, acceptable worship is thoroughly Biblical worship. What does he require of us in specific areas like giving, singing, partaking of the Lord's Supper and the decorum and spirit of our meetings together? All of these issues are addressed in the Bible. Paul told the Corinthian church that their meetings did "more harm than good" (1 Corinthians 11:17) because they were unaware of God's standards and procedures for worship. True worshipers will honor God by being attentive to his word, the truth. And they will do so with a wholehearted Spirit.

> A man worships God in spirit, when, under the influence of the Holy Spirit, he brings all his affections, appetites, and desires to the throne of God; and he worships him in truth, when every purpose and passion of his heart, and when every act of his religious worship, is guided and regulated by the word of God.[2]

For further study see John 4:1-26 and 1 Corinthians 11:17-34.

---

[2] *The International Standard Bible Encyclopedia,* 1939 ed., s.v. "Worship."

Reverence and Awe

> "Should you not fear me?" declares the Lord.
>> "Should you not tremble in my presence?
> I made the sand a boundary for the sea,
>> an everlasting barrier it cannot cross.
> The waves may roll, but they cannot prevail;
>> they may roar, but they cannot cross it." (Jeremiah 5:22)

> Therefore, since we are receiving a kingdom that cannot be shaken, let us be thankful, and so worship God acceptably with reverence and awe, for our "God is a consuming fire." (Hebrews 12:28-29)

Without a doubt, acceptable worship is a celebration of thanksgiving, but it should always be anchored in reverence and awe. To know God *is* to revere God. And to revere God is to know our place before God. Worship means "to kiss toward," or simply, to kiss the feet of God. It is total adoration, absolute respect for and complete wonder of God. It is to realize that "Great is the Lord and most worthy of praise; his greatness no one can fathom" (Psalm 145:3).

God is Creator, God is King, and God "lives in unapproachable light" (1 Timothy 6:16). He fills the universe while we—what are we? Vapor, dust, mist and clay, potsherds among potsherds (Isaiah 45:9). God holds my fragile life within his hands. He *wills* things to live and he *wills* them to die. He has the power to cast into hell and the power to forgive and exalt into heaven. Reverence and awe must pervade our worship.

We should revere God because of his grace. The psalmist declares, "But with you there is forgiveness; therefore you are feared" (Psalm 130:4). We often sing, "'Twas grace that taught my heart to fear." Forgiveness is never a right; it is never earned, never deserved. Even when we repent, forgiveness is a gift from God. We are always unworthy servants.

If we truly understood that to sin is to be worthy of hell all over again, we would better appreciate the grace of God. When we were dead in our transgressions and "by nature, objects of wrath...God, who is rich in mercy, made us alive with Christ" (Ephesians 2:3-5). He took us out of our deadness and "seated us with him in the heavenly realms in Christ Jesus" (Ephesians 2:6). When we were like newborn infants, abandoned in a field and kicking in our own blood, God passed by and said, "Live!" (Ezekiel 16:6).

Our salvation depends totally on God. Although we respond to the gospel, it is still his gospel. From first to last, God is the provider and prompter of every aspect of salvation. He opens the heart and mind. He moves us to follow his law, he inspires us to fear him, he determines the times and places and every circumstance in our conversion. It is God who invites us to church, not men, and certainly not ourselves.

> I sought the Lord, and afterward I knew
> He moved my soul to seek Him, seeking me.
> It was not I that found, O Savior true;
> No, I was found of Thee.
> NINETEENTH CENTURY HYMN (ANONYMOUS)

We should also revere God because of his holiness. In Isaiah 6, as the foundation of God's temple is quaking with power and glory, the seraphim shout, "Holy, holy, holy is the Lord God Almighty. The earth is full of his glory!" In humility, they must cover their feet, their mouths and their eyes before the resplendence. From the throne of God flow both the river of life and a river of fire. At the foot of this throne nothing is hidden from God's sight: "Everything is uncovered and laid bare before the eyes of him to whom we must give an account" (Hebrews 4:13).

The magnitude of God's grace and glory, and the invincible holiness with which he clothes himself, calls for prostration, bowing, covering, falling, trembling, even terror. Worship is a celebration, but always a reverent celebration, so that no matter what position our body is in, the heart is always on its knees. Whether we laugh or cry, sing or dance, there should always be an awareness of the presence of God. And from this awareness must proceed reverence.

For further study see 2 Chronicles 26:16-19; Ezekiel 36:24-28; Psalm 2:11, 5:7; and Deuteronomy 14:23.

PRAISE AND THANKSGIVING

> Shout for joy to the LORD, all the earth.
>   Worship the LORD with gladness;
>   come before him with joyful songs.
> Know that the LORD is God.
>   It is he who made us, and we are his;
>   we are his people, the sheep of his pasture.
>
> Enter his gates with thanksgiving
>   and his courts with praise;
>   give thanks to him and praise his name.
> For the LORD is good and his love endures forever;
>   his faithfulness continues through all generations.
> (Psalm 100)

To praise God is to exalt him, proclaim him, magnify him and glorify him. David declared, the Lord "is enthroned on the praises of Israel" (Psalm 22:3, RSV). True praise is the unashamed, utterly wonderful declaration of God's worth and blessedness. When we sing *Hallelujah!*—which means "praise the LORD"—we lift God up and let his glory shine forth. To praise is to boast in God and revel in his glory. It is to shout out for the whole world to hear and see that God is great, God is good, God is love, and God is worthy. It is deeply personal, even when you are surrounded by other disciples. He is my God, my Rock, my Shield, my Salvation, and it is my soul that boasts in him.

Thanksgiving is the sincere and grateful acknowledgment of God and for all he has given us and done on our behalf. Praise and thanksgiving overlap into each other. I thank him for his gifts, gifts that spring from the goodness of his character. But I also may thank him for who he is, his qualities or divine attributes. As the psalmist exclaims,

> I will give thanks to the LORD because of his righteousness
>   and will sing praise to the name of the LORD Most High.
> (Psalm 7:17)

Everything outside of hell is an act of God's grace. We would never stop thanking God if we could but see what he has rescued us from, let alone what he has called us *to*. Our mouths should be filled with his praise and our hearts overflowing with thanksgiving. We ought to be "overwhelmed with wonder" at what God has done for us (Mark 9:15). Miracles and countless blessing abound, from the moment of our conception in God's heart to our final glorification in heaven! His gifts, his protection, the countless deeds, the answered prayers, his attention to every detail of our lives—even in our sleep—must never be viewed as commonplace. His efforts to break us and to bless us, his divine intervention and special rescue missions ought never to be received with yawns or distracted hearts. Rather, we should accept them with the thankfulness of the blind man whose eyes were opened; with the gratitude of the thief being promised paradise just moments before his death on a cross; and with the surprise and humility of the adulterous woman as she was rescued from stoning and set free by Jesus. These people represent who we are before God, each and every one of us. Worship is the acknowledgment of these gifts, the opening and treasuring of them.

Only those whose eyes are open to God's blessings know how to properly thank him. Only those who understand the depth of God's forgiveness understand what it means to "overflow with thankfulness" (Colossians 2:7). The person who loves little or thanks little is nearsighted and blind. We need to thank God daily for our salvation, for the blood of Christ—blood that turns the immoral into virgins again, allows murderers to undergo a new birth and covers our sins like fresh fallen snow. My friend Mike Fontenot said it best: "A new snowfall can turn even a junkyard into an ice castle." This is what Jesus' blood does for us—blood so powerful, so unimaginably pure, that it allows us access to the throne of grace in the Most Holy Place in heaven itself.

Several years ago, I bought a gift for a brother and wrote him a letter in which I really poured out my heart. I wrote it to apologize and to recommit to our friendship. I really wanted to start over and have a great relationship. I bought a special card and took the time to find a special gift. A few weeks later, I was at his house, and I saw my gift lying unopened on his table. I still remember how deeply I was hurt by that one unopened gift. With God, there are countless gifts and blessings that he continually bestows on us. All that he wants, and what he deserves, is for us to be thankful and to acknowledge what he's done for us. This is crucial to meaningful worship. But sadly, there are times that I am as self-centered and oblivious as my dog, Harley. She'll devour her food and not look up even once. God have mercy!

For further study see Psalm 50:13-14, 50:23, 51:7, 69:30 and 147.

Love and Wonder

> Because your love is better than life,
>   my lips will glorify you. (Psalm 63:3)

Our worship experience needs to be filled with love and wonder. In the early church, "everyone was filled with awe" (Acts 2:43), and this should, hopefully, describe our fellowship as well. The greatest commandment, to love God with all of our heart, soul, mind and strength, really summarizes what worship is all about. Worship is the expression of our deep love for God our Savior. Like the Christmas hymn, we are filled with wonder at his love. In worship we gaze upon the blessed One, the beautiful One, the beloved One. Simply put, worship is to be amazed at God, to be amazed at the excellence of his character. We enjoy him and make ourselves vulnerable to him. People who are in love can only think about their beloved; their hearts are completely captivated. So should we be with our Savior.

> If every scroll were lifted high,
> Stretched and stapled to the sky,
> They'd not contain the things you've done.
> My Life, my All, my Beautiful One.
>
> H. K.

It must hurt God deeply when we don't love him affectionately, or when we are distant from him as Israel sometimes was. God said,

> When I found Israel,
>> it was like finding grapes in the desert. (Hosea 9:10)

But later, he could only long for her affections:

> "I remember the devotion of your youth,
>> how as a bride you loved me
> and followed me through the desert,
>> through a land not sown." (Jeremiah 2:2)

What God really desires from us is our love. This is what he deserves.

We love him "because he first loved us" (1 John 4:19). Worship is love returned. We love God for who he is and for the "indescribable gift" he has bestowed on us in Christ (2 Corinthians 9:15). In Christ, we have grace upon grace, gift upon gift, blessing upon blessing, seen and unseen, too many to count, notice or comprehend. All of this flows to us from the great love of God. In fact, God "has poured out his love into our hearts by the Holy Spirit" (Romans 5:5). Should we not also, by that same Spirit, deeply love God in return? In my opinion, this is our best and purest worship.

Worship is our kiss to God. We run to him and embrace him like a child to a parent. My favorite thing in the entire world, without a doubt, is to be tackled, hugged and kissed by my little girl, Natassja, and my son, Daniel. Sometimes my heart just turns to mush when I realize my children actually love me, their dad. I can't imagine God feels anything less than this when I run to him. This is worship.

King David lived for his time with God. Amazingly, even when surrounded by enemies, political intrigue and advancing troops, he wanted just one thing and hungered for one thing only—to seek the Lord in his temple and "to gaze upon the beauty of the Lord" (Psalm 27:4). Worship is a kind of hunger. And in worship, God speaks to that hunger.

Again, we look to Mary. Tears and affection, love and wonder, ache and hunger—this was Mary. Mary was unable to pull herself away from Jesus (John 12:3). The apostles were indignant, but Jesus was pleased. Worship is the love and wonder at the fact that I am loved by God, I am kissed by God. He is my *Abba,* and I am his delight and treasured possession. All outward forms of devotion to God—the taking of the cup and bread, the singing, the praying—mean little without fervent love. Was this not the predicament of the Ephesian church? All was motion without emotion. No matter how zealous we are, actions remain empty without love. This is the height from which we must never fall (Revelation 2:4-5).

Why me, Lord? Why was I born, why was I chosen, why was I called? Why was my heart touched? Why did I respond? Paul knows why:

> But when the kindness and love of God our Savior appeared, he saved us, not because of righteous things we had done, but because of his mercy. (Titus 3:4-5)

For further study see 1 Chronicles 29:20, John 12:1-8 and 1 John 4:7-19.

HOLINESS AND HUMILITY

If we are going to approach God, we must approach him in holiness. Consider these expressions:

> "...lift up holy hands." (1 Timothy 2:8)

> "Wash your hands, you sinners." (James 4:8)

> "Take off your sandals, for the place where you are standing is holy ground." (Exodus 3:5)

> But just as he who called you is holy, so be holy in all you do; for it is written: "Be holy, because I am holy." (1 Peter 1:15-16)

Over and over again, the Scriptures tell us that holiness is a prerequisite to approaching God.

> LORD, who may dwell in your sanctuary?
>   Who may live on your holy hill?
> He whose walk is blameless
>   and who does what is righteous. (Psalm 15:1-2)

If I had cherished sin in my heart,
    the Lord would not have listened;
but God has surely listened
    and heard my voice in prayer.
Praise be to God,
    who has not rejected my prayer
    or withheld his love from me! (Psalm 66:18-20)

Cherished and secret sin, hypocrisy, mixed motives—all of these can disqualify us from fellowship with him. The importance of "clean hands" and a "clear conscience" cannot be overstated. If we have "cherished sin" and we know that our sin hurts God, it is foolish to believe that God takes any pleasure in our worship.

When God struck down Nadab and Abihu, he said,

"Among those who approach me
    I will show myself holy." (Leviticus 10:3)

The reason that Moses and Aaron were not allowed to go into the promised land was for one reason—"you did not uphold my holiness" (Deuteronomy 32:51).

We can't fool God, nor should we deceive ourselves with the notion that his standards are lower for us today. We uphold God's holiness when we "praise him for the splendor of his holiness" (2 Chronicles 20:21) and then approach him in the holiness he expects and deserves from us. For "without holiness no one will see the Lord" (Hebrews 12:14), neither here nor in heaven.

We uphold the holiness of God, his "set-apartness," by declaring to him our utter dependence on him. This is humility. The proud cannot stand before God, just as Mary sang,

He has performed mighty deeds with his arm;
    he has scattered those who are proud in their inmost
        thoughts.
He has brought down rulers from their thrones
    but has lifted up the humble. (Luke 1:51-52)

God esteems the man or woman "who is humble and contrite in spirit, and trembles at [his] word" (Isaiah 66:2). We are but dust and ashes before God. I'm not advocating "worm theology," but rather the need to appreciate our "creatureliness" before God. We are the created and he is the Creator, and we must worship God accordingly.

Humility is learned in different ways, of course; but it is always deepened by comparing ourselves to God. For example, I don't notice my dandruff—but God numbers every hair. I can't find my car keys—yet all of creation lies open before him. I can't balance my checkbook— while God sustains every living thing. I can't pray without distraction— but God knows my every word, thought and intention even before anything is said. I live in a state of constant temptation—but God dwells in unapproachable light. I can't see behind me—but God sees through me. I can't listen clearly to even two people talking at the same time— but God hears every conversation of every man, woman and child on earth, as though each is the only one standing before him. We give galaxies and other exotic space structures boring names like M-87. We can't even catalog them all, let alone name them! God however, has numbered all ten trillion solar masses in M-87, giving each a special name and unique splendor.

> Looking to the earth
> I see the feet of all mankind,
> Dying and helpless like me.
> Chained with stubborn root
> To a small and fragile planet,
> Broken by our own humanity.
> Looking to the stars
> I see the face of God,
> Strong, luminous,
> Eternally free,
> Peeking over the edge of an infinite sky
> And laughing at his own invincibility.
>
> H. K.

Understanding who we are before God is one of life's most important lessons. Consider Job, one of God's great worshipers. In a crisis of
despair, he shot question after question toward his God. But God did not
answer even one. Instead, he fired back a hundred more: "Where were
you when I laid the earth's foundation?...Can you loose the cords of
Orion?" (Job 38:4, 31). Job was stunned into silence. He covered his
mouth and finally, remarkably, was at peace. This, I presume, is a lesson
God meant for all of us.

For further study see Luke 1:46-54, Job 38-42:6, Hebrews 12:14-15
and Leviticus 10:1-3.

SELFLESS AND UNASHAMED

How hurtful it must be when we are ashamed of God. Worship
should be the declaration that God is our all, that he is the only thing
that matters, that we love him more than life itself. David was
unashamed in his worship; he loved praising God in the presence of
others. It wasn't enough that he loved his God, but he wanted everyone
else to know it. He wrote about his love for *El Shaddai*, sang about it,
danced to it and flat out gloried in it. He was uninhibited in his dancing
and unashamed to declare his love for God among his friends, amidst
the congregation, to the nations, in the presence of his enemies, and
even before the "gods."

We should be *God*-conscious, not *self*-conscious as we worship.
The sinful woman who burst in upon Jesus' dinner with a Pharisee was
blessed by God as she followed the instincts of her heart. She poured
out not just oil, but her soul. Another time, his apostles rebuked Mary
for "wasting" the perfume in the alabaster jar, but Jesus honored her
for her deep devotion. Such public displays of affection are never
condemned by God when they are sincere.

We must be proud of God, as he is of us. In his word he tells us that
we are the ring on his finger, the apple of his eye, his treasured
possession. This truth should cause our light to really shine in the
assembly. God wants us to be fully engaged with him, with all of our
bodies and with all of our emotions. In the Scriptures they bowed in

worship, lifted hands, danced, shouted, fell and jumped. These are the ways that individuals praised God in private and in public.

We, too, need more expressiveness: extolling, singing, amens, the lifting of hands, exuberance and kneeling. Marilyn and I miss worshiping with the disciples in Africa. Every element of the worship service— the expressiveness, the harmonies, the energy and sheer physicality— was so inspiring! While in Lagos, I remember chancing upon an all-night prayer meeting of about a dozen brothers. The room was rocking and the tropical heat didn't matter a bit. I could hear the rumbling from outside. I went in and found the brothers dancing and rejoicing like David before the Lord. They had completely and utterly given themselves over to the worship of God—and it was amazing! I wish I wasn't so shy. Of course, we do need to worship with decency and order, but that doesn't imply a stifling formalism. Michal despised David for his reckless abandon, for disrobing before the slave girls, for "humiliating" himself in front of others. But, as someone wryly observed, Michal had to face a different kind of music herself— barrenness. We must never be sloppy or cavalier in our approach to God, but there should be an uninhibited exalting that takes place when we worship him wholeheartedly.

For further study see 1 Chronicles 15:25-29 and 2 Samuel 6:12-23.

CELEBRATION AND JOY

> My mouth is filled with your praise,
>   declaring your splendor all day long. (Psalm 71:8)

> Shout for joy, O heavens;
>   rejoice, O earth;
>   burst into song, O mountains!
> For the LORD comforts his people
>   and will have compassion on his afflicted ones.
> (Isaiah 49:13)

> For the LORD takes delight in his people;
>   he crowns the humble with salvation.

> Let the saints rejoice in this honor
> and sing for joy on their beds.
> May the praise of God be in their mouths. (Psalm 149:4-6)

Worship is celebration of God and the life he has given us. There are times in the Scriptures when worship was a parade-like spectacle. David and the Israelites celebrated with all their might before God and sometimes the joy of their celebration could be heard outside the city walls. At times the ground shook.

A Christian is one whose cup overflows with the joy of celebration. Part of worshiping under the old covenant involved attending annual festivals, and God's people were to keep these feasts with joy. Our gospel is "good news of great joy" (Luke 2:10)! Read Psalm 150 and you will understand that worship is the party of all parties. Read Revelation 19 and be amazed at the thunderous shouts of joy, the resounding celebration of heaven. Contrary to popular belief, heaven is a noisy place!

For further study see Isaiah 61:10; Psalm 84:1-2, 9:1-2, 35:9-10, 28:7 and 16:9-11.

DECLARATION AND DEPENDENCE

> "And now, LORD God, keep forever the promise you have made concerning your servant and his house. Do as you promised, so that your name will be great forever. Then men will say, 'The LORD Almighty is God over Israel! 'And the house of your servant David will be established before you." (2 Samuel 7:25-26)

Worship is a declaration. We remember the great works of God and we declare them. The exhortations of Peter to remind...to refresh...to recall (2 Peter 1:12-13, 3:2) all find their place in worship.

After the apostles were flogged and warned, they prayed and declared God's sovereignty over all the nations (Acts 4:24-30). King Asa declared that he was absolutely helpless before God, that he was utterly dependent upon him (2 Chronicles 14:11). Jehoshaphat gathered all of Judah together—men, women and children—to declare their helplessness before God. At the head of his army were singers, not soldiers! (See 2 Chronicles 20:21-22.)

Throughout the Bible we find worshipers who appeal to the promises that God has made. They "remind" God of his own promises, and because of these reminders, which are declarations of faith in him, God acts. This kind of declaration upholds God's greatness and is an appeal, a jealousy, for his glory alone.

By definition, worship is always a form of dependence.

> As the eyes of slaves look to the hand of their master,
>   as the eyes of a maid look to the hand of her mistress,
> so our eyes look to the Lord our God,
>   till he shows us his mercy. (Psalm 123:2)

We are powerless, but God is all-powerful. We are helpless, but he gives help to the helpless. Like David, Israel's king, we are "poor and needy" before him (Psalm 40:17). We admit that he alone gives victory to kings, that we do not trust in ourselves, in horses or in chariots. We do not trust in the world. We do not ally ourselves to the nations around us. We do not seek their strength in battle. We do not turn to them when we are afraid. We give it all to God. We look only, always to him.

Hezekiah spread out a scroll of Sennacherib's threats before God. He entered the temple and essentially said to God, "Read it for yourself. You are being defamed and I am jealous for you. We are weak; you are strong" (see 2 Kings 19:14-16). And then God acted.

> So the Lord saved Hezekiah and the people of Jerusalem
> from the hand of Sennacherib king of Assyria and from the
> hand of all others. He took care of them on every side.
> (2 Chronicles 32:22)

> "Do not be afraid or discouraged....For the battle is not yours,
> but God's." (2 Chronicles 20:15)

For further study see Psalm 50:15, 27:1, 28:7, 9:13-14; 2 Samuel 7:25; 2 Chronicles 14:11, 16:7, 9 and 20:5-15.

If we earnestly desire to become true worshipers of God, we must begin with the ABCs. As we grow and become more adept with their use, our expressions of worship will never fail to stir our hearts. More importantly, we will not fail to stir the heart of our God.

12

First, Best, All, Only

G od is worthy of the very best things we have—not just firstfruits but "the best of the firstfruits" (Exodus 23:19). He is not the Lord of our leftovers, nor is he is a secondhand Savior. He is God Almighty, and he is to be revered.

Nowhere is this truer than in our worship. We must sing with all our hearts; preach as though declaring the very words of God; teach as those who are in the presence of God; and pray with faith, conviction and passion as we lead our congregations before the throne of God. We must plan our services with skill, purpose and deliberation. Those who lead singing should do so with a joyful and radiant countenance, inviting and engaging the rest of the congregation. Ushers must be punctual and serve faithfully, with a firm but kind and attentive manner, remembering that even the temple had its temple guards! Those who lead our thoughts in communion should strive to portray Christ as crucified before our very eyes. Their aim must be to draw our attention to Christ, not away from him—as irrelevant or meager anecdotes are sure to do.

Solomon's grave warning must be heeded today:

> Guard your steps when you go to the house of God. Go near to listen rather than to offer the sacrifice of fools, who do not know that they do wrong.
>
> Do not be quick with your mouth,
> do not be hasty in your heart
> to utter anything before God.

God is in heaven
    and you are on earth,
        so let your words be few.
As a dream comes when there are many cares,
    so the speech of a fool when there are many words.

...Much dreaming and many words are meaningless. Therefore stand in awe of God. (Ecclesiastes 5:1-3, 7)

Irreverence and flippancy are always trying to rear their ugly heads in the midst of our times of worship. We must identify and eliminate anything that would dull our veneration and awe of God. Otherwise we, too, will offer the "sacrifice of fools."

We give our best to God because that is how God has given to us. We give with heart and soul because he gave his heart and soul. We love him "because he first loved us" (1 John 4:19). God had but one Son to offer us, and that is what he gave—an inexpressible and indescribable gift. And not only did he give us Christ, but along with him, he graciously gives us all things. Christ himself became poor to make us rich, to make us kings.

God's desire to lavish his best upon us can be seen in the blessing that Moses pronounced on the descendants of Joseph:

"May the Lord bless his land
    with the precious dew from heaven above
    and with the deep waters that lie below;
with the best the sun brings forth
    and the finest the moon can yield;
with the choicest gifts of the ancient mountains
    and the fruitfulness of the everlasting hills;
with the best gifts of the earth and its fullness
    and the favor of him who dwelt in the burning bush.
Let all these rest on the head of Joseph,
    on the brow of the prince among his brothers."
(Deuteronomy 33:13-16)

"Precious," "deep," "best," "finest," "choicest"—these are the ways that God gives to us. These must be the ways that we give to God.

OLD SCHOOL

The Old Testament clearly taught that Israel was to give their best to God. Everything had to be pure, best, finest, holy. Jews were expected to give sacrifices of fat and blood. Offerings to God fell into two categories: holy offerings and most holy offerings. Every firstborn male belonged to him, whether man or animal. The only acceptable sacrifices were those without blemish or defect. When property was confiscated from enemy nations, everything that could be burned in the fire had to be burned in order to purify it before offering it to God. If it could not withstand the fire, it needed to be washed. The tabernacle and temple were built with only the finest materials. Their design came from God's own mind and spirit. For the temple, exquisite carvings on exquisite materials were overlaid in gold. It was beautiful through and through! The most skilled and talented craftsmen were to build it. Those who were gifted in music were to excellently lead and train other singers in excellence.

What is God's message in all of this for you and me? What must our standards of worship be under the new covenant if the Old Testament was only a shadow? Back then, the blood of animals was offered to make the worshipers ceremonially (outwardly) clean, but today we can worship with our consciences cleansed through the blood of Christ. Our worship is to be pleasing, acceptable and fragrant. We must offer God the sacrifices worthy of his great and glorious name, approaching him with a spirit of excellence, willingness, cheerfulness, reverence and awe. Following are just a few of the principles we can glean from worship under the old covenant.

Never Empty-Handed

In worship we come to give, and each gift is measured by the heart of the giver. We cannot all give equally, but we can all give the best of what we have—if not a lamb, then a pigeon; if not a pigeon, then a grain offering (Leviticus 5:7,11). My singing may be off key, but I can still make a joyful noise unto the Lord! I may be older and not physically as exuberant, but I can still overflow with thanksgiving.

Quality, Not Quantity

In Jesus' parable, the Pharisee went on and on about himself, but the tax collector merely uttered a sentence. One pleased God; the other didn't. As Jesus observed people at the temple, many were throwing in large amounts of money. One gave only two small coins. She pleased God; the others did not. God notices not only how, but why we worship. Are you serving him wholeheartedly?

Freely and Joyfully

"God loves a cheerful giver" (2 Corinthians 9:7)—someone who wants to worship him, who desires to be with him, who seeks to please him. He is thrilled when we have consecrated and prepared ourselves to meet with him in worship. "I don't feel like it," you may say. So what? God demands that you give your best effort anyway. Every day, every single day, Nehemiah appeared before Xerxes and was cheerful because he stood before the king. The occasion when his countenance was sad was a onetime exception, not the rule, and that exception drew the attention of the king. If Nehemiah could stand joyfully before a pagan king, day after day, then we can worship with joy before our God.

EXCELLENCE AND ENERGY

The book of Malachi offers one of the clearest glimpses into the lifeless soul of halfhearted worship. Of course, the Jews who had resettled their homeland after the captivity had a form of worship. They shed tears. They sacrificed blood. They gave stuff, lots of stuff. But in the end, it was all repulsive to God—blemished animals, blissless worship, contemptuous sniffing and a general attitude of feeling burdened by the whole affair. They gave because they *had to,* but they didn't even give all of their tithes. And how did God feel about this?

> "Oh, that one of you would shut the temple doors, so that you would not light useless fires on my altar! I am not pleased with you," says the LORD Almighty, "and I will accept no offering from your hands."

> ..."Cursed is the cheat who has an acceptable male in his flock and vows to give it, but then sacrifices a blemished animal to the Lord. For I am a great king," says the LORD Almighty, "and my name is to be feared among the nations." (Malachi 1:10, 14)

These Jews had just been released from seventy years of captivity, and what were they focused on—honoring God, or keeping stuff for themselves? They were out of touch and out of their minds, full of motion without emotion, without heart. Their ignorance, as demonstrated by the questions they asked, is embarrassing.

> "How have you loved us?" (Malachi 1:2)
>
> "How have we shown contempt for your name?" (Malachi 1:6)
>
> "How have we defiled you?" (Malachi 1:7)
>
> "How have we wearied [you]?" (Malachi 2:17)
>
> "How are we to return?" (Malachi 3:7)
>
> "How do we rob you?" (Malachi 3:8)

God answers by saying that they had made his table contemptible.

> "When you bring blind animals for sacrifice, is that not wrong? When you sacrifice crippled or diseased animals, is that not wrong? Try offering them to your governor! Would he be pleased with you? Would he accept you?" says the LORD Almighty.
> ..."And you say, 'What a burden!' and you sniff at it contemptuously," says the LORD Almighty.
> "When you bring injured, crippled or diseased animals and offer them as sacrifices, should I accept them from your hands?" says the LORD. (Malachi 1:8, 13)

They also said things like,

> "It is futile to serve God. What did we gain by carrying out his requirements and going about like mourners before the LORD Almighty?" (Malachi 3:14)

Whether these people literally spoke these words or only thought them is not important. The point is what God read in their hearts during their acts of worship. His opinion of their worship is what really mattered, and amazingly—from priest to common man—they all seemed to be ignorant of what God expected from them. To worship God acceptably, we must start by making two decisions.

Honor God

Set your heart on honoring God. This is not difficult; it is a simple decision. In Indianapolis, our number one goal this year is to have deep, meaningful, awesome worship services. Recently, we set aside a Friday evening to learn some new songs. Bill Culpepper, who had just moved to our congregation from the Triangle church in North Carolina, was leading us. At first the singing was okay, but then it became listless and unenthusiastic. Bill stepped up to the microphone and gently charged us to make a decision to give our best in singing. That one act changed everything. Even though we were learning a new song, we sounded alive and angelic. All it took was one simple decision: I will sing out; I will set my heart.

Fear God

Second, set your heart on fearing God. When there is no fear of God, we are not excellent and energetic in worshiping him. Again, hear the words of Malachi:

> Then those who feared the LORD talked with each other, and the LORD listened and heard. A scroll of remembrance was written in his presence concerning those who feared the LORD and honored his name.
>
> "They will be mine," says the LORD Almighty, "in the day when I make up my treasured possession." (Malachi 3:16-17)

From this, we see that God looks at the whole group of worshipers but takes note of those who fear and reverence him. He writes their name down on a scroll. It is not merely those who attend church or who claim to be worshiping God who are his, but rather the *true* worshipers become God's treasured possession.

WHO'S ON FIRST?

God must be first in our lives. The book of Haggai offers another clear example of this point. Returning after seventy years in captivity, the worship of God was not the top priority for those in Haggai's day. *They themselves* were their top priority. They could not find time to rebuild the temple of the Lord, but somehow managed to rebuild their houses. They wanted the best and first things for themselves, and they neglected to build up the house of God, their place of worship. What was the result of this neglect? God blew down their houses, put holes in their wallets and refused to bless them. It was a critical situation, but thankfully, one that could be fixed.

God himself moved the spirit of the high priest and the people to begin rebuilding the temple. The outcome was astonishing.

> "From this day on, from this twenty-fourth day of the ninth month, give careful thought to the day when the foundation of the LORD's temple was laid. Give careful thought: Is there yet any seed left in the barn? Until now, the vine and the fig tree, the pomegranate and the olive tree have not borne fruit.
> "From this day on I will bless you." (Haggai 2:18-19)

The lesson here is simple. When we put God first, the turn in events becomes so dramatic, the blessings so apparent, that we can look to the exact month, the exact day, the exact moment when things became different. "Give careful thought to your ways," says the Lord (Haggai 1:7). When they looked back on that day from future months or years, they would realize clearly that it was the very day when God began to bless them. When God is first in worship, he takes pleasure in this and is honored. When he is second, we have only ourselves to blame for the barrenness.

Secondhand, second rate, second best. All these things are sacrilege in worship. Is God the Lord of my leftovers or the Lord of my all? Does he hold sway over my whole heart, or is halfhearted worship the best he sees from me?

PRACTICAL QUESTIONS

1. When I sing, do I mean what I say? "All to Jesus I surrender."[1] "Love so amazing, so divine, demands my soul, my life, my all."[2] Do I mean it, or is it flattery and false promises?

2. Am I sincerely grateful, deeply thankful, fully focused on the cross of Christ when I take communion? Does it move me more now, over time, or less? Am I being silly or flippant or given to distraction? Am I engaged in worship at this point? Do I truly recognize the body of the Lord, or am I busy planning other things?

3. When the collection plate is passed, am I giving to God or to a plate? Am I giving like a son or daughter of God or a son of Caesar? Am I truly sending them on their way "in a manner worthy of God"? (3 John 6). Do I realize that my giving to the poor is giving to Jesus? (See Matthew 25:40.) To show kindness toward the poor is to show kindness toward God (Proverbs 14:31, 19:17). Have I been kind to God? Is it with conviction that I give, or is it just Corban or tradition or what is expected?

4. Do I really care about how I sing, or do I not even have a songbook to bring, or maybe forget it once too often?

5. Is my preaching powerful, full of God's word, logical, persuasive, relevant and prepared? Do the hearts of our hearers burn within them as we break open the Scriptures? Or is it just the same old, same old? Shame on the lazy expositor!

---

[1] Lyrics by Judson W. Van DeVenter, "All to Jesus I Surrender," *Songs of the Kingdom, 2nd ed.* (Woburn, Mass.: Discipleship Publications International, 1999), song 474.

[2] Lyrics by Isaac Watts, "When I Survey the Wondrous Cross," *Songs of the Kingdom, 2nd ed.* (Woburn, Mass.: Discipleship Publications International, 1999), song 382.

6. Are we teaching our children like we really believe the Bible? That Jonah really was swallowed by a fish? That Adam and Eve really were the first two parents? That there really was a flood that overwhelmed the earth? Am I persuasive? Am I engaging? Am I challenging? Do I carefully answer their questions and meet their needs, or am I boring and uninteresting? It is a sin to bore people with the Bible when we know we can do better.

7. Am I habitually late to church, always sitting at the back, careless about interruptions and causing distractions? Once in a while, each of us will be late—maybe even to help someone in need on the way to church as the Samaritan did—but the problem of habitual lateness is not your clock or the traffic or acts of kindness. The problem is irreverence.

8. Do I really pay attention to the Scriptures as though they are the oracles of God? Am I seeking to apply them? Do I have the same spirit as Samuel, "Speak, Lord, for your servant is listening" (1 Samuel 3:9). The words of Scripture are no less God's words than if he spoke them from Mount Sinai, than if the ceiling opened and God were to declare them in person. (See Nehemiah 8:1-6.)

9. Have I come to spend myself in the fellowship for the sake of God's people, or am I selfish and preoccupied with things of the world? "God is not unjust; he will not forget your work and the love you have shown him as you have helped his people and continue to help them" (Hebrews 6:10).

10. When the songleader or other worship leaders stand in front and are ready to commence, do I stop fellowshiping, or am I the exception? I'm not saying we need to be abrupt, but there is a powerful message that is sent, to ourselves and our friends, when we stop as soon as possible and stand at attention, ready to worship God. It is quite awesome, really.

11. There are various moods in worship. Every service will be a bit different. Some are more of a celebration, some more subdued, depending on the Scriptures, the circumstances, the choice of songs and so on. However, it should be unnecessary for our

worship leaders to have to cajole us to get us fired up, to be more giving, to say more amens. Just decide to give your whole heart from the start. It's that simple.

12. Do I regularly come to worship services, or am I in the habit of missing the assembly of the saints? Am I eager to assemble, to meet with God and his people, or do I make excuses that are meager? Do the sniffles keep me away? An overtime job? Tiredness from staying out too late? Cal Ripken, who played in 2,632 consecutive baseball games, will rise on Judgment Day to condemn many of us on this point. (See Luke 11:31-32.)

13. A helpful tip: memorize the order of the books of the Bible so you can follow along. You'll save a ton of time and convict or inspire your guests without saying a word.

14. Am I aware of my surroundings when I come to church? Am I attentive to the needs of my brothers and sisters and to our guests? "Can I help you find a seat?" "Would you like to share my songbook with me?" "Here, let me help you take your children to the class and get settled." Do I serve by helping with a crying infant? Do I notice those who are sitting alone or needing encouragement? Maybe I need to step up and help others to pay attention or encourage my kids to be more giving in the fellowship or more lively in their singing.

15. Lastly, have I judged myself—examined my heart—before I take the Lord's Supper? Am I holding a grudge? Do I need to confess my sins? Am I really conscious of one body, the church, feasting on one body, the Savior? The Lord's Supper is a gift from God, an act of mercy. God knows that we are forgetful, and we need to thank him for giving us this memorial. The Lord's Supper is not just a part of our service; it is central to our service—it is why we gather. If any moment is to be sacred, it must be this moment.

God knows that we are frail, that many of us are babes in Christ, that we are mist and vapor, given to distraction. Because of this, God will only demand from us what he knows we can give. He understands if a husband or wife had an argument on the way to church (not good, but it happens). He knows when our children are up all night because they are sick, or if I am a single parent, trying to get three kids ready and out the door on time. God is merciful and gracious. His throne is a throne of grace. When my daughter draws me a picture of a house, it is squiggles, upside-down letters, pictures pasted up and down with sparkles and strings, and copious amounts of Elmer's Glue. And when she says, "Here, Daddy!" that glue is on my clothing, my hands and my shirt. And what do I say? "Wow, for me? You did that? Thank you so much!" Then I hug her and then I praise her, "You're amazing. What great colors. You're fantastic. You're gonna be an artist—no, a ballet dancer, a gymnast, a black belt in Tai Kwon Do, Princess Leah, Queen Amidalah *and* an artist!" The point is, glue or not, her picture would have stuck to my hand. I am fired up because she has given me something from her heart. She might not have drawn the Taj Mahal, but she is only four years old, and her work is meaningful to me.

God is patient and kind. He is not looking for perfection in our worship. No, but what I am talking about is our willingness, attention, sincerity, integrity and wholeheartedness in worship. Whether ushering, preparing communion cups, cleaning the trays, teaching the children, leading a prayer, reading from the Scriptures, or engaging in fellowship, we must do the very best we can, with all the joy and conviction that we can muster. It is a decision. We choose to set our hearts to honor and to fear God.

13

THE LORD'S DAY

'**O**n the Lord's Day," wrote John as he introduced the book of Revelation, "I was in the Spirit" (Revelation 1:10). So began a most powerful time of worship, awe and inspiration. For every Christian, Sunday—the Lord's Day—should be a special day, a greatly anticipated time of heartfelt participation. It's the *Lord's Day;* the day we come together as Christ's body, to honor and worship the Father. It is the day we corporately remember the cross and celebrate the resurrection of our Lord. It's a day that *must* be great, every week, whether you are new to the faith, or a disciple of twenty years participating in your 1,040th service. Our zeal for God's glory and his kingdom needs to burn especially bright on this "holy day"—a day uniquely set apart to focus on him. We must be on our guard against the human tendency to let worship degenerate into boring and vain repetition that blocks out the glory of God, leaving our hearts unchanged. Instead, our Sunday services need to be fresh, alive and "in the Spirit"—worship that is without question "in spirit and in truth" (John 4:24). Nothing less is worthy of the God we serve.

Writing this book came about as a result of wrestling with these issues in the Indianapolis church. Our Sunday services were generally good (subjectively speaking), but not always great. Many of the members here have been disciples for more than fifteen years, some for twenty. As I began to preach and teach about the need for true worship, many began to admit (or confess) that their Sunday worship was not as inspiring or edifying as they knew it ought to be. We had fallen into a rut, individually and collectively, of habitual, often mindless singing, stale praying, and shallow, distracted fellowship. As members of God's spiritual temple, built to house the very Spirit of God, this clearly was not right! We began to focus on the heart and soul of true worship, and to make inward and outward changes as the Spirit taught and reminded us. It has been refreshing to everyone to see our worship services come alive with new fervor and zeal. Hopefully, God is encouraged, too. What follows are some of the lessons we have learned and are striving to put into practice.

FIRST THINGS

Although little is said in the New Testament about the specific format and style of a first century worship service, we can glean much from the book of Acts and from the epistles about the heart and priorities of their worship. We know that they were devoted to the reading and preaching of Scripture and to prayer and that their primary focus on the Lord's Day was to commemorate the death and resurrection of Jesus through the Lord's Supper. Their communion services sometimes took place as part of an *agape* (a "love feast," Jude 12), and more attention was paid to the condition of the worshipers' hearts than to the format of the meal itself (1 Corinthians 11:17-34).

If we could travel back in time to the first century, we would probably be surprised by differences in the Jewish style of worship in the Jerusalem church and the Gentile flavor of the church in a city like Rome. The lack of specific references to the type of singing, preaching or praying done by the church indicates that these "issues" were not meant to be issues; what mattered most was that God was glorified through sincere worship, sound doctrine, godly lives and a unified fellowship. In everything, the gospel—"of first importance" (1 Corinthians 15:1-3)—was to be preached and celebrated. And in all the preaching, praying, prophesying and fellowshiping, Christ was to be exalted as Lord of all.

The same must be true today. We can have different styles and preferences in worship, as long as we remain true to these priorities and remain unified with one another. Consider John the Baptist and Jesus. You will be hard put to find two leaders with more different approaches to their ministries. One sang a dirge, the other played a flute (Luke 7:32), but both preached a message of repentance to enter the kingdom of God: two contemporaries, two completely different lifestyles, but perfect unity.

Sunday Worship

The fourteenth chapter of 1 Corinthians deals with problems that the church encountered when it placed an emphasis on speaking in tongues rather than on love, order and edifying the church. However, with proper attention given to these concerns, it would seem that the first Christians were free to develop forms of worship as they saw fit. What were the elements of a first century worship service?

There was Scripture reading.

> Until I come, devote yourself to the public reading of Scripture, to preaching and to teaching. (1 Timothy 4:13)

They read the Law and the Prophets as well as the teachings of the apostles.

> After this letter has been read to you, see that it is also read in the church of the Laodiceans and that you in turn read the letter from Laodicea. (Colossians 4:16)

There were sermons and discussions.

> On the first day of the week we came together to break bread. Paul spoke to the people and, because he intended to leave the next day, kept on talking until midnight. (Acts 20:7)

There was much singing. The early church sang psalms that were expressive of every type of prayer, hymns to teach her members the theology of the newly emerging church and spiritual songs that stirred emotions as well as the intellect.

> Let the word of Christ dwell in you richly as you teach and admonish one another with all wisdom, and as you sing psalms, hymns and spiritual songs with gratitude in your hearts to God. (Colossians 3:16)

There were prayers.

> Therefore confess your sins to each other and pray for each other so that you may be healed. The prayer of a righteous man is powerful and effective. (James 5:16)

> I urge, then, first of all, that requests, prayers, intercession and thanksgiving be made for everyone—for kings and all those in authority, that we may live peaceful and quiet lives in all godliness and holiness. (1 Timothy 2:1-2)

There were congregational amens.

> If you are praising God with your spirit, how can one who finds himself among those who do not understand say "Amen" to your thanksgiving, since he does not know what you are saying? (1 Corinthians 14:16)

> And so through him the "Amen" is spoken by us to the glory of God. (2 Corinthians 1:20)

There was a confession of faith.

> Fight the good fight of the faith. Take hold of the eternal life to which you were called when you made your good confession in the presence of many witnesses. (1 Timothy 6:12)

Everyone came to participate.

> When you come together, everyone has a hymn, or a word of instruction, a revelation, a tongue or an interpretation. All of these must be done for the strengthening of the church. (1 Corinthians 14:26)

There were collections.

> Now about the collection for God's people: Do what I told the Galatian churches to do. On the first day of every week, each one of you should set aside a sum of money in keeping with

his income, saving it up, so that when I come no collections will have to be made. (1 Corinthians 16:1-2)

There were physical actions. They lifted up hands.

I want men everywhere to lift up holy hands in prayer, without anger or disputing. (1 Timothy 2:8)

There were greetings and there were benedictions.

Grace and peace to you from God our Father and the Lord Jesus Christ. (1 Corinthians 1:3)

All the saints send their greetings. (2 Corinthians 13:13)

And they greeted each other with a holy kiss.

All the brothers here send you greetings. Greet one another with a holy kiss. (1 Corinthians 16:20)

Greet all the brothers with a holy kiss. (1 Thessalonians 5:26)

True Worshipers

How can we make our worship services more powerful, more worshipful and above all, more pleasing to God? First of all, each of us must do his or her part. As one of the many parts of the body, I will either strengthen or weaken our corporate worship. My attitude and heart as I prepare for Sunday worship is crucial. Am I eager to worship God and to be with his people? Is coming to church a burden or an incredible privilege? The Jews of the Old Testament were expected to travel to Jerusalem three times a year, in order to worship God and keep the festivals. The attitude expressed in Psalm 122: "I rejoiced with those who said to me, 'Let us go to the house of the Lord,'" was simply the expectation.

In this public national worship the truly devout Jew took his greatest delight, for in it were inextricably woven together, his patriotism, his sense of brotherhood, his feeling of solidarity, his personal pride and his personal piety.[1]

Does this describe *your* spirit on Sunday morning?

In China, the Middle East and in many struggling Third World countries, disciples often risk arrest or imprisonment to meet together. Others walk many miles in tropical heat in order to worship with the church. My family and I have lived in India and in Africa—and these disciples are real, their stories unexaggerated. What excuses do you make for being lazy or lackadaisical about coming to church?

True worshipers come to church eagerly, with hearts prepared to give. Much of that preparation starts the day before, clearing our hearts of any unconfessed sin, resentment or bitterness that could contaminate our fellowship with God or others. (See Matthew 5:23-24.) We may need to call a brother or sister, or work through an issue face to face that has brought hurt or division into our relationship. Spouses, how was your heart this week toward your husband or wife? We can't truly give to God (or to others) if our hearts are blocked with bitterness or anger.

Another aspect of preparation includes spending some great time with the Lord before we go to church. Having communed and prayed in your private devotional time, your public worship will be deeper and more meaningful. I think specifically of the "Songs of Ascents" (Psalms 120-134), as well as other psalms, written to prepare the individual's heart for communal worship. The psalmists understood that our hearts need confession, forgiveness, praise and anticipation if we are to "connect with God" at the temple.

As we come into the "sanctuary" (be it a theater, church building, hotel or school), our countenance needs to be Christlike: warm, giving, loving, encouraging. Being in a bad mood, being critical or even being "into yourself" is unacceptable for a disciple. We come together to encourage and edify one another; each member's contribution is essential. Giving up your seat, reaching out to visitors, going out of your way to greet the weak, elderly or physically challenged members— these are all ways to give as Jesus would.

---

[1] *The International Standard Bible Encyclopedia,* 1939 ed., s.v. "Worship."

A fellowship full of giving disciples will be abuzz with energy and love and will make a huge impact on visitors. Not long ago, we received a letter from an anonymous visitor, saying that she had enjoyed the service—but that nobody had reached out to her, either before or after the meeting. I wondered if I had been one of those who simply overlooked her that day. We pray that she gives us another chance, and that next time she finds us radically different!

As we encouraged one other in Indianapolis to come prepared, some great suggestions surfaced. Singing spiritual songs on the way to church is a favorite. It takes the edge off of a rushed morning, especially in a busy household, and lifts everyone's spirits. Our vocal chords get warmed up, too, which helps for the opening song. Many families have a group prayer on the way, and we all try to leave earlier so that we can avoid rushing in at the last minute. These simple practices can make a huge difference in the way we come into the worship service.

As the service begins, our attitude must be reverent, as we turn our attention to those who are leading the worship. This means that the first song, rather than serving as an opportunity to finish conversations and greet a few more people, needs to be the real beginning of our worship service. When the songleader gets up, the fellowship needs to hush: It is time to worship God Almighty. Leaders, especially, take note—we can be the guiltiest when it comes to using the first few songs to tie up unfinished business. Imagine that you are coming into the very presence of God, into the Holy of Holies, and let every tongue be silenced— except to sing his praises.

Marilyn and I have always believed that the heart of a congregation can be felt through its singing. Some of our most memorable moments of angelic choruses and "joyful noise" have been in Africa. In our opinion, the stirring, harmonious songs of South Africa are among the best in the world; and the clapping, dancing and excitement of the West African churches is the most rhythmic, by far. All of us have our own personal taste in music. Some like spirituals, others the classic hymns, still others the "hand-clappers." Whatever your preference is, let nothing keep you from singing with *all* your heart, even if the current song is not your favorite. Becoming "all things to all men" (1 Corinthians 9:22) includes learning to respect and appreciate the wide variety of musical styles we experience in our diverse fellowship. Bring your songbook to church and *sing*—sing with all your heart, every word of every song. Some of us need to loosen up, too—lifting up our hands as we sing or even falling on our knees in humility, letting God's Spirit move us as we worship. I am not talking about unruly worship, or actions that are done to draw attention to ourselves. (Often, this does nothing more than "weird out" our guests!) However, there are times we have all been deeply moved during the congregational singing, perhaps wanting to drop quietly to our knees, but we allow self-consciousness to stifle what may be the prodding of the Holy Spirit. There are no "commandments" on this, but David's example alone, "a man after God's own heart," shows us a worshiper who was uninhibited and expressive before God.

LEADING THE WAY

Those who lead us in worship need to really *lead us in worship*. Whether songleading, praying, preaching or speaking, all must be done prayerfully and excellently, in service to God. (See 1 Peter 4:10-11.) The songleaders (and songwriters) that are seen in the Old Testament—Asaph, the sons of Korah, Ethan the Ezrahite—were not "airheads" or "spacey" as a result of being artistic; they were warriors, prophets, city-builders, counselors to the king. They were godly, spiritual men who used their talents to serve God's people. Our songleaders and singers, likewise, ought to be skillful and spiritual men and women. Since singing is such an important part of our worship, songleaders should be innovative and creative, willing to learn and to teach new ways to keep our singing fresh and inspirational. "Three songs and a prayer" can get stale, especially if it's the same old three songs we've been singing all year! How wonderful it is to have songleaders who surprise us with new songs or even new ways of singing old favorites.

Those who lead in prayer and the communion must also lead with meaningful, well-thought-out words that express our hearts toward God. Preparation is the key. We have enjoyed some powerful public prayers and communion messages in Indianapolis recently as we have strived to take it higher for the Lord. When we keep our focus on Jesus, always filling our messages with him and with the Scriptures, hearts will be changed, and he will be glorified.

Just as every aspect of the physical temple had significance and meaning, every aspect of our worship service needs to be meaningful. Our contribution—the giving of "our" money back to God—is also an act of worship. I have often admonished the church to "give more than a Happy Meal" to our weekly contribution for the poor. Every act of giving is pleasing to God when we give cheerfully and generously. There are many who find further ways to give generously: by ushering, setting up the sound system, filling the baptistery with water, preparing the communion bread and trays, providing water for the speakers to drink, and gathering the "lost and found" articles week after week. These unsung heroes are serving the church in ways that will be noticed and remembered forever (Matthew 10:42). Let us be thankful for each of them and remember to show our gratitude for all they do.

Even when the service "ends," it is not really over. The fellowship we engage in after the last song is still part of our worship. Great fellowship means giving to one another: lingering longer to talk, getting to know someone new, initiating new ways to serve and be together, building friendships of depth and substance. According to Romans 12 (the entire chapter) our "spiritual act of worship" includes giving to each other in a myriad of ways, being hospitable, being devoted to one another in brotherly love and being willing to associate with people of low position. These are all endeavors that can and should be part of our celebration on the Lord's Day.

NOT WITHOUT EFFECT

Whenever we meet together, whether in thousands, hundreds, dozens, or groups of just a few, the Lord will be with us (Matthew 18:20). My wife, Marilyn's, first introduction to the kingdom was a Sunday meeting of just three people—and she was the solitary visitor! It could have been a forgettable, insignificant morning, a "failure" in the eyes of men—but instead, it changed her life eternally. Why? Because even in that tiny group of two disciples (Paul, my partner in the gospel, and me), she felt the Spirit of God in our simple, reverent worship. The Scriptures were read (the covenant of blessing and cursing from Mounts Ebal and Gerizim!); the gospel was preached; the Lord was praised and entreated in prayer. Even the contribution message, based on most of 2 Corinthians 8 and 9, was convicting and life-changing: she emptied her pockets that day! Poor girl.

True worship is powerful and humbling. It draws people to the Lord. It allows us to lose ourselves in the adoration of Jesus. It can't be faked.

Christ is, of course, the reason we worship; the reason we *can* worship. He is our lamb and our high priest. His blood enables us to stand freely, unashamedly, confidently, joyfully, even boldly, in the presence of God. We are baptized in his name. We assemble in his name. It is the Lord's Supper we participate in. It is the Lord's Day, the first day, the day of the resurrection, the day of the firstborn. For his name's sake, let us give our very best each week when his special day comes.

14

TREASURE

HE SAID TO THEM, "THEREFORE EVERY TEACHER OF THE
LAW WHO HAS BEEN INSTRUCTED ABOUT THE KINGDOM OF
HEAVEN IS LIKE THE OWNER OF A HOUSE WHO BRINGS OUT
OF HIS STOREROOM NEW TREASURES AS WELL AS OLD."
MATTHEW 13:52

Make new friends, but keep the old.
One is silver and the other gold.
TRADITIONAL

If all that I have been saying about God is true, then our times of worship ought to be the highlight of our days. Going through the motions of a stale routine may appease the conscience of a legalist, but it will never bring us deeply into the presence of God or bring him the praise that he deserves. We are enjoined to do whatever it takes to focus our hearts and minds on the majesty of God.

Here are a few practical suggestions that I hope will enrich your walk with God and deepen your personal worship experience. Some are quite simple, others quite radical. I have tried most of these, but need to try all of them once more! If necessary, start with repentance. Decide to have a deep conviction to worship God in a richer and worthier manner. "Rend your heart and not your garments" (Joel 2:13). Only sincere determination will make us better worshipers. And better worshipers are the kind that God seeks.

1. Of first importance, always return to Jesus Christ and the Gospels.

   > As soon as all the people saw Jesus, they were over-
   > whelmed with wonder and ran to greet him. (Mark 9:15)

   John said, "I suppose that even the whole world would not have room for the books that would be written" about him (John 21:25). We must "consider" him, "set [our] minds" on him, "fix our eyes" on him (Hebrews 12:2-3; Colossians 3:2).

2. Begin a Bible study on the attributes and qualities of God. "Great is the LORD and most worthy of praise" (Psalm 145:3). Better yet, if you can afford it, buy a Bible and mark it up, backward and forward. Collect these scriptures, organize them and in your praise and worship to God, go through them.

3. Learn new songs. "Sing to the LORD a new song" (Psalm 96:1). There are thousands of songs to be learned and enjoyed. Don't wait for new ones to be learned in the church; find your own. If you discover a song you like or believe would inspire the fellowship, suggest it to your church leader or your songleader.

4. Buy or borrow tapes. There are all kinds of music tapes and CDs in Christian bookstores. I have bought many recently. It is so much better for the soul to listen to these songs than to listen to the radio. They elevate our thoughts and help us to take every thought captive for Christ—not to mention that they can help calm our nerves, even in the chaos of traffic.

5. In your personal quiet times, use your songbook or hymnal for meditation. Meditation on the words of familiar songs speaks to your heart differently when you are alone. This will also make your singing of them richer in public worship. How many times have you sung "Amazing Grace"? Only recently the words "twas grace that taught my heart to fear" leapt off the page for me. It *is* amazing.

6. Learn to read music (Psalm 33:3). This may seem like a difficult task, but it's doable. Reading music helps us to sing more

expressively and more truly. When songs are sung correctly in their parts, they can move from boring to breathtaking.

7. Write a love letter to God. David probably composed hundreds, if not thousands, in his life, as did his son Solomon. Write at the epochal moments and the "just because" moments. You don't have to show what you have written to anyone—it's your love offering to God. I have found this to be a good way to refresh my memory and fill my heart with what God is doing around me. But more, it brings him immense satisfaction.

8. Sing in your morning devotional. David said, "I will sing and make music. Awake, my soul! Awake, harp and lyre! I will awaken the dawn" (Psalm 57:7-8).

9. Dance. Dancing is a form of worship. Personally, I'm a poor dancer, but who cares? David danced before the Lord with all his might. We are encouraged in Psalm 150 to "praise him with tambourine and dancing." You may want to try this by yourself, especially if you've never done it before!

10. Make a thank-you list (Psalm 103:1-5). Write down a sincere and meaningful thank-you list of the specific ways you are blessed; then praise God for each one.

11. Retrace all the aspects of your conversion. In other words, look back and see how God worked in the small things and big things, through circumstances and conversations and scriptures. How did God seek you and find you?

12. Ponder and enjoy the creation. God is proud of his entire creation. Every living thing teaches us something unique about God. "Consider how the lilies grow" (Luke 12:27). "Lift your eyes and look to the heavens" (Isaiah 40:26). "Can you bind the beautiful Pleiades?" (Job 38 and 39). Nature is richer, profounder and more mysterious than any of us could possibly imagine. There are hidden geometries, subtle textures and patterns, rich pallets of colors, the gift of sound, the wonder of spirals, the eyes of dragonflies, the shape of a leaf, the ingenuity of each animal. Jesus said, "Consider the lilies," and from his own considering, he

realized a flower is more splendid than all of Solomon's robes. David considered and marveled at God's ability to "open [his] hand and satisfy the desires of every living thing" (Psalm 145:16).

Go on nature hikes. When we were in South Africa, we would take hikes with our son Daniel and have contests to see who could find the coolest bug or the best flower or the wildest color. It's a great way to spend time as a family, as well as teach them about their Creator.

Study anatomy—especially human anatomy. Indeed, as David proclaimed,

> I praise you because I am fearfully and wonderfully made;
>   your works are wonderful,
>   I know that full well. (Psalm 139:14)

Most of us have no idea where a spleen is, much less the medulla oblongata!

If you're really getting into it, take a chemistry course. I did. I took a semester of chemistry at Old Dominion University. I love chemistry—the mystery of atoms and the way they interact, the molecules they produce—it's almost magical. God is so phenomenal. Maybe you can study biology or physics or astronomy or read books on gravity or the theory of special relativity or maybe the phenomenon of light. Is it a wave? A particle? Both? I have— no kidding—spent months on end thinking about the gift and richness of light. Impossible you say? Not really. When asked what he was going to do after his general theory of relativity, Einstein said, "I will spend the rest of my life trying to understand light." To explore and examine the works of our Creator is to deepen the worship of our Creator.

13. Pray and sing through the Psalms. Use them as your own prayer book, your prayer hymnal. This is something Douglas Jacoby shared with me years ago. Use the Scriptures as your divinely-inspired prayer list. Memorize the Psalms. Sing from your heart what David wrote and sang.

14. Continue your study of the subject of worship. I read my Bible three times with this one subject in mind. It has awakened me to a whole area of my Christian life that I neglected for too long. It has begun to change my life right now, and I know it will profoundly change my life in the future. It is also beginning to change the depth of our worship as a church in Indianapolis. We still have a long way to go, but the journey, like our entire Christian life, is from glory to glory.

15. Freewill offerings. How about doing something extraordinary for God? Something you're not required to do? Maybe give up something you really want to do just to be able to spend special time with God. I'm not saying cancel plans that you've already made, but maybe reserve a Saturday night for a special date—just between you and God. Or give a large gift to the poor in honor of the Lord. Do anything that goes beyond what is being asked of you with the motivation to do it for God.

16. Another excellent study would be the word meanings of worship in Greek, in Hebrew, in English and in Latin.

17. Lift your hands. Some of us may feel uncomfortable lifting our hands in worship. We are a little embarrassed, a little self-conscious. But it is enjoined in the Scriptures again and again. There is a vulnerability to this gesture, a welcoming, like the response of a child to a father. Maybe you can do this in your own quiet times, then you will feel more comfortable doing it in public.

18. Be honest with God. Be as real and as open as you can be. You don't have to pretend before God. You don't have to pray in the King James language. Just be honest and pour out your soul. That's what a relationship is all about.

19. Teach your kids about worship (Psalm 8:2, Exodus 12:25-28). The very act of teaching our children increases our own understanding of worship. God was known as *"the Fear of Isaac"*—I wonder why! We also need to teach our children about reverence and the fear of God. We must be attentive to their prayers, listening to their expressions and "tuning in" to their concept of God. We must

teach them to revere God's name, guard against flippancy and help to develop a greater awareness of his presence.

20. Read the book of Leviticus, every word of it. The majesty of God is the theme. Imagine being a priest of Israel. I also suggest a study of the various temples in Scripture.

21. Learn from the great worshipers in the Bible like Abraham, David, Asaph, Moses, Nehemiah, Ezra, Mary or Anna.

22. Write a song. Compose your own music. Create some lyrics. We need so many more songs, songs that lift our hearts to God, songs that recount what God is doing in our movement and in the kingdom around the world. If it is for public worship, it needs to be excellent and should be written skillfully. But if that is not your gift, do it anyway—for yourself and your toddler or maybe your spouse.

23. Consider the heavens. I am a certified star junkie. "Oh God, make small the old star-eaten blanket in the sky, that I might fold it round me and in comfort lie."[1] The silence and vastness of the night sky calm me and allow my heart to soar on wings. Clearly, the stars are one of God's greatest gifts to us. I bought my first "big" telescope in India, an inexpensive cardboard tube—but it worked! I was so fired up to see the shadow on Venus. In Pretoria, I would drag disciples onto our roof to see Jupiter's moons and Saturn's rings. Go to the library and read books about the stars and our universe, or visit a university observatory and take your date there. However you do it, just do it. There are thousands of breathtaking pictures thanks to the Hubble telescope. Go online and be amazed. God himself said, "Lift your eyes and look to the heavens: Who created all these?" (Isaiah 40:46).

24. Watch nature shows with your family.

25. Learn hymns sung by Christians from other nations. One of the greatest blessings of being able to travel and to have lived in several cities abroad, was to hear the Christians sing new songs, with new lyrics. It is wonderful to hear God glorified in another culture, with different harmonies and scales.

---

[1] Thomas Ernest Hulme, "The Embankment."

26. Compose your own communion message. Whether you are able to share it publicly or not, just do it. What would you say if you did have the opportunity?

27. Embark on a study about some of the more mysterious aspects of God's being, such as his triune nature, the Incarnation or the mystery of his absolute sovereignty and our free will.

28. Take a personal retreat, a day or two, or a hike in the woods just to spend some special time with God. Christ himself said, "Come with me by yourselves to a quiet place and get some rest" (Mark 6:31).

29. Invite some Christians over just to sing and praise God (Psalm 106:2).

30. Go out of your way to do something for the poor and needy. Worship and justice go hand in hand. Without giving and without justice there can be no sincere worship. In fact, this is one of the most revealing and challenging studies in the Scriptures. To honor the poor is to honor God.

31. Memorize entire prayers and passages on worship—maybe even long passages. Sixteen years later, I remember memorizing 1 Chronicles 29:10-14 with Jim McCartney, back in the early days of Boston. And I remember how great it was to get on our knees and pray that noble prayer of David.

32. Devote one Sunday as a full-fledged day of worship for you and your family. Enjoy a full day of simply delighting in God, thanking him, reading scriptures and enjoying one another's company. In short, don't waste your energy or effort on anything except the things of God on that day.

33. Buy a book or two on worship, or go to the library and study what others have written. It's always amazed me that for ten or fifteen bucks I can buy something that somebody has studied out and worked on for years. That's a good deal if you ask me!

34. Do a study on the various expressions of worship found in the Psalms. For instance: "I ascribe, I lift, I exalt, I exult, I tell, I declare, I praise, I boast, I meditate, I remember," etc. (See the appendix.)

35. Have a Passover evening. This can be a deeply meaningful experience. I have done this for the last ten years in the churches or family groups that I have been part of. We usually sing and pray for a few hours, reading scriptures from Exodus and the Passover to the passion of Christ. We usually have a simple Middle Eastern type of meal, not a traditional Seder, but with egg, olives, humus, lamb, bitter herbs, etc. We do this every Good Friday, retracing in Scripture and song the last day of Christ from supper to resurrection.

36. Learn the stories behind some of our classic hymns. The man who wrote "Amazing Grace" was once a murderer and slave trader. The man who wrote "Be Still, My Soul" lost his entire family in the Atlantic Ocean.

37. Meditate on these five passages concerning the suffering and death of Jesus: Psalm 22, Isaiah 53, Matthew 27, Philippians 2 and Revelation 4 and 5.

38. Deepen your Bible study skills. The psalmist said, "The law from your mouth is more precious to me than thousands of pieces of silver and gold" (Psalm 119:72). Concerning the prophets, Peter said they "searched intently and with the greatest care" (1 Peter 1:10). I don't mean reading the Bible more. I mean reading the Bible better, with more care and deliberation. Apart from accuracy, we must learn to engage our emotions and imagination when we study. And add to this the practice of meditation—which is really only longer stretches of concentrated thinking, chewing over the word of God. Picture a cow ruminating in a field, and you will have a good idea of what I am talking about.

39. Consider a special detailed study of these subjects or scriptures: Psalm 119; how Christ himself respected and used the Scriptures; Psalm 145-150; the love of Jesus in the Gospels; the book of Hebrews; worship and the reconstruction and restoration of the temple (Ezra, Nehemiah, Malachi, Haggai, Zechariah).

40. Try reading the Bible, especially the Psalms and prophets, in different translations.

41. Have an *Upside Down* party. In Virginia Beach, we rented a classic, refurbished, old-style theater and had our largest Sunday gathering ever for the viewing of this powerful musical.

42. Study the lives of the great "desecrators" of idols in the Bible. These men not only restored the true worship of Jehovah, but were ruthless in expunging all forms of idolatry as well. Check out men like Josiah and Jehu to get a taste of this Old Testament "sport of kings." Have we demolished the idols of our lives? Are we crucified to the world?

43. Read a good commentary on Hebrews. If you're not sure which one, get some input from your minister or an elder or teacher in your congregation.

44. Preachers, our messages need to excite and stimulate and deepen the faith of God's people. We must faithfully proclaim the whole counsel of God, give them deep and meaty sermons that are expository and textual, not just topical in nature.

45. Finally, cleanse your heart. Each one of us is the temple of the Spirit of God. If we cherish sin in our heart, God will not hear us. It is impossible to have a deep relationship with God if we have secret sins. Do we tolerate those things we should be ashamed of? Only with pure hearts and clean hands can we draw near to God.

This is in no way meant to be an exhaustive list, nor are all of these ideas guaranteed to make your times of personal worship automatically more meaningful. Ultimately, you must work at your own relationship with God. Hopefully you will find these suggestions helpful in creating your own list of tried and true aids to deeper worship. And as we bring out of our storerooms "new treasures as well as old," God will see a freshness and vitality in our hearts that encourage him each time we approach him.

15

Transformed Before Him

Worship that is true and sincere not only glorifies God, but also transforms his worshipers from deep within. God honors, rewards and empowers his worshipers, for as we behold God "with unveiled faces" (2 Corinthians 3:18), we become like him—not only in heaven but here on earth. His desire is that we "become mature, attaining to the whole measure of the fullness of Christ" (Ephesians 4:13); that we be "made new in the attitude of [our] minds" (Ephesians 4:23); that we "be conformed to the likeness of his Son" (Romans 8:29); and that we "put on the new self, created to be like God in true righteousness and holiness" (Ephesians 4:24). This happens as we "fix our eyes on Jesus" (Hebrews 12:2), as we "set [our] minds on things above" (Colossians 3:2), and as we focus on no one but Jesus and "consider him" (Hebrews 12:3). The blessings that God bestows on worshipers are far too numerous to list, but here are a few to establish the point and to encourage our hearts.

Worship Glorifies

God wants to be glorified in his people, and he wants Jesus to be honored as a result of those who wear his name. The more we change and become like Christ, the more glory is given to God. In fact, our metamorphosis is described as going from one degree of glory to another. And the more we change, the more praise our Lord receives.

> Now the Lord is the Spirit, and where the Spirit of the Lord is, there is freedom. And we, who with unveiled faces all reflect the Lord's glory, are being transformed into his likeness with

> ever-increasing glory, which comes from the Lord, who is the
> Spirit. (2 Corinthians 3:17-18)

Here, using the term "unveiled," Paul is referring to the result of Moses' times with his God. When he would come into the presence of God, whether on the mountain or in the tent of meeting, his face would become radiant. Although he was not aware of this phenomenon at first, the rest of Israel was. The sight was so mysterious—eerie even—that Moses had to wear a veil in order not to frighten the people. What kind of effect has your radiance had on others, as you are transformed by your deeper and deeper relationship with God? (See 2 Corinthians 3:7-18.)

We will never rise above our understanding of God. "The most important thing about a man is what comes into his mind when he thinks about God."[1] Our concept of him is crucial as we worship. Indeed, we become like the object of our worship. Of course, this is the very expectation of God our Father—to be like him in all we do. Our transformation is from glory to glory, becoming as much like God as possible.

> Be holy, because I am holy. (1 Peter 1:16)

> "Be perfect, therefore, as your heavenly Father is perfect."
> (Matthew 5:48)

> Forgive as the Lord forgave you. (Colossians 3:13)

> Be imitators of God. (Ephesians 5:1)

> Live a life of love, just as Christ loved us. (Ephesians 5:2)

WORSHIP PURIFIES

We are commanded to "get rid of all moral filth" (James 1:21), to "put to death...whatever belongs to [our] earthly nature" (Colossians 3:5), and to "be holy, because I am holy" (1 Peter 1:16). Many of these directives involve outward action by us. Nonetheless, true sanctification is from

---

[1] A. W. Tozer, *The Knowledge of the Holy* (New York: HarperCollins Publishers, Inc., 1975), 1.

the inside out and is, on its deepest and most fundamental level, a work of God. When I worship, God softens my heart, making it sensitive again to the repulsiveness of sin. The taste of sin loses its flavor. The material world loses its grip. Clinging self-centeredness is banished, and the desire for this world evaporates, as it did for Jesus while he was tempted in the desert: "All this I will give you," said the devil; "Worship the Lord your God, and serve him only," answered Jesus. (See Matthew 4:9-10.)

A renewed awareness of and disdain for sin come about as a result of worshiping God. This happens in several ways. As we consider the cross, sin and its effects should become vividly apparent, causing us to want nothing to do with it. Also, focusing on God as we worship purifies us. As the apostle John put it, "Everyone who has this hope in him purifies himself, just as he is pure" (1 John 3:3). If the *hope* of seeing God purifies us, then the worship of God also purifies us.

Through God's Spirit, we are purified inwardly. We realize that God is our Father, that he is among us, and that we are to not touch anything unclean.

> Since we have these promises, dear friends, let us purify ourselves from everything that contaminates body and spirit, perfecting holiness out of reverence for God. (2 Corinthians 7:1)

WORSHIP CLARIFIES

Worship is looking to God alone, as David did: "[I] beheld your power and your glory" (Psalm 63:2). As we do so, we gain a better perspective of what is real and important, in addition to a greater measure of trust in God.

Job was confronted by an unimaginable series of crises and tragedies. He was a deeply righteous man who, in the midst of his anguish, became clouded in his thinking and theology. When God showed himself to Job and convinced him of his sovereignty and wisdom, Job was humbled and *satisfied*.

Uzziah was a good king, a great king even. He gave his nation stability and peace. He was an agriculturist, an architect, an exquisite planner and a powerful warrior. When he died, many must have wondered what would become of God's people. "In the year that King Uzziah died," God showed himself to Isaiah (Isaiah 6:1-8). In reality, the true king never stopped reigning.

As Revelation 2 and 3 relate, the church of the first century was about to undergo pressures and trials never before experienced. How would they endure? Why was God letting this happen? The answer is dramatically given in the opening verses of Revelation 4 as the curtain is pulled back and we see God still on his throne, still in charge. They needn't worry.

Asaph had one of the most privileged positions in Israel. He was a prophet, a gifted psalmist and a leader in the worship at the temple. Yet even he started to lose perspective and fell into merely *working* in the temple instead of *worshiping* in the temple. He was overcome with bitter struggles and envy. Asaph explained in embarrassing detail the sad condition of his heart in Psalm 73: *Why me? Why do they have all the fun? Life is so hard. Poor me, etc.* He later came to his senses and confessed, "I was senseless and ignorant; I was a brute beast before you" (Psalm 73:22). How did he change?

> When I tried to understand all this,
>   it was oppressive to me
> till I entered the sanctuary of God;
>   then I understood their final destiny.
> (Psalm 73:16-17)

In the quiet of the temple, God spoke to his heart. In the presence of the eternal God, eyes are opened, the fog and stupidity are lifted, and we regain an eternal perspective.

A similar incident occurred in the life of the Babylonian king, Nebuchadnezzar. But instead of envying the world, he usurped God's glory by declaring that he *was* the world. Just like that, he became like a cow. His sanity was restored—and so is ours—only as he "raised [his] eyes toward heaven" (Daniel 4:33-34).

In worship we are to "set [our] hearts on things above, where Christ is seated at the right hand of God...not on earthly things" (Colossians 3:1-2). As we focus on Christ and praise him for his life, his blood and his grace, the mirage of earthly pleasures will evaporate. The grip of the world loses its power. Hell and heaven come into focus. The answers to questions like "Why?" and "What is life all about?" become even clearer.

Have you ever had thoughts like these: *Why don't they have problems—why is it only me? Why couldn't I be a movie star? Why does he get all the breaks? Why is she getting away with this? Why can't I be rich? Life is so easy if you're not a Christian. Look at them—so free, so much fun, always happy. Why do I have to go to church and give away my money, serve the poor and stay up late to help people with their marriage problems? Why do I have to get up early? Blah, blah, blah.* Well, you aren't alone! Asaph had similar thoughts, and his way out was to worship God. Worship helps us to see things as they truly are: The world is rubbish, a bit of dung, a coin for Caesar. We have much to be grateful for, and God has never stopped being in charge.

WORSHIP FORTIFIES

The Bible makes it clear that those who look to God are strengthened and empowered by him. God uses the greatness of his being to empower us. It is not an accident that the last verse in Luke's gospel describes a scene in which the disciples were "continually at the temple, praising God" (Luke 24:53). When Luke takes up the story again in the first two chapters of Acts, the disciples were again praying and worshiping God. While they were in this position of humility before God, the Spirit came on them in power. Some time later, as they worshiped God and declared with conviction his absolute sovereignty, "They were all filled with the Holy Spirit and spoke the word of God boldly" (Acts 4:31). In chapter 13, the disciples in Antioch were worshiping when God's Spirit set apart Paul and Barnabas for their missionary task. And again in chapter 16, when Paul and Silas found themselves in prison for their faith, they sang hymns to God, and God answered by sending an earthquake.

Worship fortifies us and produces courage and peace in our hearts. When we see God, we understand his challenge to us: "Who are you that you fear mortal men, the sons of men, who are but grass?" (Isaiah 51:12). We are emboldened because we realize God is with us like a mighty warrior, a dreaded champion. We have the confidence of David as he faced Goliath: "You come against me with sword and spear and javelin, but I come against you in the name of the LORD Almighty, the God of the armies of Israel, whom you have defied" (1 Samuel 17:45). We have the calm assurance of Stephen, who died as a martyr, seeing Christ standing at the right hand of God. We have the peace of Elisha, who did not waver when surrounded by Arameans because he knew that all around him were fiery chariots—chariots that were not summoned, but were already there. His servant Gehazi responded in fear because he did not see them. Elisha uttered the words that all great men and women of God utter because of his unshakable conviction of God's sovereignty and presence: "Don't be afraid" (2 Kings 6:16). As we worship, as we look to God and declare his glory, as we remind ourselves of his power and his deeds, worship fortifies our souls. It empowers us.

When Christ himself was tempted in the wilderness, his consciousness of God shone through in all of his responses to Satan's ploys. *It is the word of God we must feed on....Don't put God to the test....Worship God and serve him only.* And how did he return from this difficult time of tempting? He returned "in the power of the Spirit" (Luke 4:14). As we concern ourselves with God, and only God, God will empower us, even as he empowered his Son.

To be engaged in worship is the safest place we can be. Here we are in the shelter of *El Shaddai.* Here we are surrounded by songs of deliverance. Here God surrounds us with his unfailing love.

WORSHIP SIMPLIFIES

In worship we realize that we possess the pearl of great price, Jesus Christ. Nothing else in this world matters more. As the psalmist said,

> Whom have I in heaven but you?
>> And earth has nothing I desire besides you.
> (Psalm 73:25)

In worship we declare that God is our all and all that we need. Paul could say, "One thing I do" (Philippians 3:13). Mary chose "what is better" (Luke 10:42). David said,

> One thing I ask of the LORD,
>> this is what I seek:
> that I may dwell in the house of the LORD
>> all the days of my life,
> to gaze upon the beauty of the LORD
>> and to seek him in his temple. (Psalm 27:4)

I love this poem by Frederick William Faber:

> Only to sit and think of God, oh what a joy it is.
> To think the thought, to breathe the name, earth has
>> no higher bliss.
> Father of Jesus, love's reward, what rapture it will be,
> Prostrate before thy throne to fall, and gaze and gaze
>> on thee.

Worship has a way of just simplifying things for us, giving us perspective, satisfying our souls "as with the richest foods" (Psalm 63:5). "I would rather be a doorkeeper in the house of my God than dwell in the tents of the wicked," wrote Asaph (Psalm 84:10).

WORSHIP TERRIFIES

Worship is a declaration of our utter dependence on God. For this reason, worship is also an act of war. The demons tremble when we pray in Jesus' name. Indeed, Christ has given us authority to trample Satan under our feet (Romans 16:20). Those who worship declare war in Jesus' name and terrify the enemy.

The Scriptures recount several battles that were won when God's people simply worshiped him and expressed a jealousy for his glory alone. When Jehoshaphat and the people of Judah received word that a mighty army was gathering against them, they stood before God and confessed that they were helpless. Even the little children were there. In a moving display of desperate faith, the king prayed,

> "We have no power to face this vast army that is attacking us.
> We do not know what to do, but our eyes are upon you."
> (2 Chronicles 20:12)

Assured by God that he would take the battle into his own hands, Jehoshaphat positioned priests at the head of the army to sing of God's enduring love "and to praise him for the splendor of his holiness" (2 Chronicles 20:21). Because of this trust in God and jealousy for his glory, they never had to lift their swords, but God struck down the enemy for them.

God delivered his people in a similar way in Hezekiah's day. (See Isaiah 36-37.) Sennacherib was a wicked king who led a wicked nation. The Assyrians were the "Klingons" (villains) of the Old Testament. They surrounded Hezekiah. They blasphemed God. They boasted in their great strength. They tried to terrify the hearts of the people by telling them they would have "to eat their own filth and drink their own urine" (Isaiah 36:12). The Assyrians were a bloody, ruthless people. In the face of such opposition, what could Hezekiah do? He personally took the letter from Sennacherib to the temple with him and spread it out before God. It was then that he prayed his prayer about keeping their eyes on God alone (2 Chronicles 20:12). And how did God answer? He sent one angel, who destroyed 185,000 Assyrian soldiers.

King Asa was another of Judah's kings who chose to depend on God in prayer rather than trust in his own strength. Asa had more than a half million soldiers who were all brave and skilled. But even with this well-equipped army, listen to Asa's prayer when a Cushite army marched out to meet them in battle:

> "Lord, there is no one like you to help the powerless against
> the mighty. Help us, O Lord our God, for we rely on you, and

> in your name we have come against this vast army. O LORD,
> you are our God; do not let man prevail against you."
> (2 Chronicles 14:11)

And what does God do? He routs the enemy.

Worship terrifies the enemies of God. Check out this example: Paul had a reputation in the demon world. When the seven sons of Sceva tried to exorcise a demon from a man in the city of Ephesus, the demon—before pouncing on them and beating them to a bloody pulp—said, "Jesus I know, and I know about Paul, but who are you?" (Acts 19:15). True disciples of Jesus have a reputation in the demonic realms among "the rulers,...the authorities...[and] the powers of this dark world" (Ephesians 6:12).

Our worship really does make the enemy tremble. Here we destroy, even demolish, strongholds. Here we bind every thought that sets itself up against God. In worship we are jealous for God's glory. In worship we pray in Jesus' name. This is the realm in which demons are bound and placed under our feet.

> The God of peace will soon crush Satan under your feet.
> (Romans 16:20)

> He replied, "I saw Satan fall like lightning from heaven. I have
> given you authority to trample on snakes and scorpions and
> to overcome all the power of the enemy; nothing will harm
> you." (Luke 10:18-19)

At the name of Jesus, angels mount, swords flashing, ready to do the will of God.

WORSHIP BEAUTIFIES

I continue to be amazed when I see women who have come back from the mission field, not ragged but shining. They just seem so beautiful and so radiant! This beauty, I believe, comes from surrender and love. A radiant countenance also comes from the worship of God. The Bible teaches that "those who look to him are radiant" (Psalm 34:5).

There is a special beauty that God bestows on those who learn to trust in him, who are submissive to him. Peter relates that godly women of the past, like Sarah, made themselves beautiful by being submissive to their husbands.

There is a light in our eyes, a peace that passes understanding, a joy that is inexpressible, which all beautify us when we revere God. Outward beauty is a gift from God, but inward beauty is an even greater gift. "Charm is deceptive, and beauty is fleeting; but a woman who fears the LORD is to be praised" (Proverbs 31:30). This is true beauty.

> The LORD their God will save them on that day
>> as the flock of his people.
> They will sparkle in his land
>> like jewels in a crown.
> How attractive and beautiful they will be! (Zechariah 9:16-17)

WORSHIP SATISFIES

Heaven will provide the ultimate satisfaction for our souls. We will drink from the river of the water of life and be nourished by the trees in paradise. But we should not think that we must wait until then to experience true satisfaction. God wants to satisfy our souls here and now. We are most satisfied—and God is most glorified—when he is our all. David describes the fulfillment that comes as we seek after God.

> O God, you are my God,
>> earnestly I seek you;
> my soul thirsts for you,
>> my body longs for you,
> in a dry and weary land
>> where there is no water.
> I have seen you in the sanctuary
>> and beheld your power and your glory.
> Because your love is better than life,
>> my lips will glorify you.
> I will praise you as long as I live,
>> and in your name I will lift up my hands.

> My soul will be satisfied as with the richest of foods;
>> with singing lips my mouth will praise you.
> On my bed I remember you;
>> I think of you through the watches of the night.
> Because you are my help,
>> I sing in the shadow of your wings.
> My soul clings to you;
>> your right hand upholds me. (Psalm 63:1-8)

God is our living water, our bread of life. He satisfies our souls as with the richest foods. We gaze upon his beauty and are delighted. We experience the pleasure and wonder of his acceptance and the peace of his forgiveness. Our yearnings are met, our hunger is satisfied, our cup overflows. This is not true of feeble, halfhearted singing and worship, but in real, sincere worship in which we open ourselves up to all that God is and has for us. This world leaves us hungry and thirsty. It cannot meet our longings and our deepest spiritual needs. Only through God can this take place, and it takes place when we worship.

WORSHIP UNIFIES

One of the richest blessings of worship is the unity it creates in our local fellowship and in the kingdom worldwide. Unity is sacred to God. It is a testimony before the world and the authorities in the heavenly realms of his power and manifold wisdom.

> This mystery is that through the gospel the Gentiles are heirs together with Israel, members together of one body, and sharers together in the promise in Christ Jesus....His intent was that now, through the church, the manifold wisdom of God should be made known to the rulers and authorities in the heavenly realms, according to his eternal purpose which he accomplished in Christ Jesus our Lord. (Ephesians 3:6, 10-11)

Christ prayed for his disciples to be one even as he and his Father are one. This is a very high standard, and corporate worship is clearly the greatest means of attaining it. We see this principle of worship and unity exemplified in both the Old and the New Testaments.

Under the Old Covenant

In the Old Testament, the tabernacle/temple was the very heart and soul of Israel. Every man, woman and child was a part of this blessing. The worship of God was to invade every aspect of the life of Israel. During the period of wilderness wandering, the tabernacle was in the physical center of the camp, surrounded on all sides by the twelve tribes, with the Levites in the inner circle. Its very design and rituals created unity among the tribes. The tabernacle and temple belonged to all, and were built by all with the gifts from all and the talents of all, for the sacrifice of all. When Aaron went into the tabernacle, he was to wear a breastplate over his heart bearing the names of all twelve tribes.

The feasts and the festivals also had the benefit of unifying the nation, once it spread out after the conquest of the promised land. All qualified males from every tribe were commanded to appear before the Lord at the appointed season or risk being cut off from the community. These feasts fostered unity and reminded all of them of their privileged status as a nation. They worshiped the one true God, read from one Law and had one high priest and one house of worship, the place that bore God's name. As a nation, they were God's "treasured possession" (Deuteronomy 7:6). There was none other like them "on the face of the earth."

Under the New Covenant

In the New Testament, we are the temple of God, a dwelling in which God lives by his spirit (Ephesians 2:20-21). We are one household, one body, one bride, one nation, one royal priesthood, and with one heart and mouth we are to glorify God. Worship establishes and deepens this oneness. We have one mediator and "one God and Father of all, who is over all and through all and in all" (Ephesians 4:6). We have been saved by the same grace, covered by the same blood, filled with one and the same Spirit, baptized into one body by that Spirit (1 Corinthians 12:13). Every Christian is sacred to God, each a magnificent temple, a special creation (1 Corinthians 6:19, 12:14-18).

Through worship, we are reminded of our equality in Christ. The least among us is the greatest. The weakest are to be treated with special honor. True worship upholds the dignity and glory of each disciple.

> My brothers, as believers in our glorious Lord Jesus Christ, don't show favoritism. Suppose a man comes into your meeting wearing a gold ring and fine clothes, and a poor man in shabby clothes also comes in. If you show special attention to the man wearing fine clothes and say, "Here's a good seat for you," but say to the poor man, "You stand there" or "Sit on the floor by my feet," have you not discriminated among yourselves and become judges with evil thoughts? (James 2:1-4)

It is very easy to be awed by the rich and famous, the well-to-do and the "together," neglecting the humble among us, even in the fellowship. Fine clothes and gold rings—so what? Who cares? Do they love Jesus? That's all that matters. All the rest is dung and delusions.

> Lowborn men are but a breath,
>   the highborn are but a lie;
> if weighed on a balance, they are nothing;
>   together they are only a breath. (Psalm 62:9)

We must be prouder of the least Christian among us than of anyone who belongs to the world. We must be more drawn, more charmed, more in awe of a child of God than of the most attractive movie star, the richest stockbroker or the most powerful president or king who does not love Jesus. We must feel this way whether our brother or sister is doing well spiritually or not, whether he or she is the greatest or the least. To look down on our brother, to not wait for him, to say "sit at my feet" or "stand over there," not only brings embarrassment to him but also to God and to his church. To show favoritism is to sin against Christ and to worship in an unworthy manner. Sincere worship guards our hearts against this grievous evil. We are one in the Lord.

One of the lowest points in my Christian life, when I felt like "the least" in the fellowship, came when my family and I were living in Pretoria, South Africa. Although surrounded by awesome brothers and sisters, I went through a very difficult time, entangled in sin and doubt and depression. Like Nebuchadnezzar, I also had a momentary lapse of reason—feather headed, long fingernails, eating grass like a cow—or so it seemed. I wanted to surrender and quit.

Then Douglas Arthur called. Douglas lives with the conviction that when a brother is down, you shouldn't walk over him; instead, you should reach down and pull him up, again and again if you have to, and help him with all you have to help. That's all I have to say—he helped me get a second wind, gave me a second chance, extended grace and hope. Douglas is my hero and I love him. I love the kingdom; I love the brotherhood of believers; and I want to always love the weakest among us—which could be you or me!

Only God is capable of bringing such unity into the kingdom. We of every tribe and language, people and nation worship *one* Lord and Savior. We sons and daughters of one Father in heaven, kneel to worship with one mouth, as one body, with one heart and soul. As we worship, we establish and strengthen our oneness. In an unbroken circle of love and affection, we have been adopted and called to the feast of Father, Son and Spirit, where God is over all, through all and in all.

> How good and pleasant it is
> > when brothers live together in unity!
> It is like precious oil poured on the head,
> > running down on the beard,
> running down on Aaron's beard,
> > down upon the collar of his robes.
> It is as if the dew of Hermon
> > were falling on Mount Zion.
> For there the Lord bestows his blessing,
> > even life forevermore. (Psalm 133:1-3)

WORSHIP RECTIFIES

Finally, worship reconciles relationships by convicting us of our sin. Can I really partake of the Lord's Supper with a good conscience if I withhold forgiveness from a brother? We are to forgive one another "just as in Christ God forgave you" (Ephesians 4:32). And again Jesus warns, "unless you forgive your brother from your heart" (Matthew 18:35), "your Father will not forgive your sins" (Matthew 6:15).

On the other hand, maybe someone has something against you. Jesus again calls us to action:

> "Therefore, if you are offering your gift at the altar and there remember that your brother has something against you, leave your gift there in front of the altar. First go and be reconciled to your brother; then come and offer your gift." (Matthew 5:23-24)

When we worshiped in Johannesburg, from time to time we would have a break in the service before taking the Lord's Supper in order to have a time of confession and reconciliation. Although this lasted only five or ten minutes, it was very enriching, very unifying.

Worship should and does melt our hearts toward the saints. As we look around and see those for whom Christ died, it must move us to love each other deeply. I can sing until I'm blue in my face, give all I have to the poor, and offer my body to the flames, but if I have not love for the least of the saints, I am nothing and my worship is useless. "If anyone says, 'I love God,' yet hates his brother, he is a liar. For anyone who does not love his brother, whom he has seen, cannot love God, whom he has not seen" (1 John 4:20). It is impossible.

All of us together—very different in gender, skin color, social status, education level, talents, gifts, language and culture—form one body. This is the beauty and the power and the glory of the kingdom. We have one God and Father, one Lord and Savior. All of us, joined and held together by every supporting ligament, rise to become a dwelling in which God lives by his Spirit. And from this dwelling, "with one heart and mouth" (Romans 15:6), we glorify God.

These are just a few of the blessings that God bestows on us as individual Christians and as a community of worshipers. Looking up to God, gazing upon his beauty, concentrating on his character, opening our hearts and engaging our minds, surrendering in obedience to his will—these are the things that glorify our Father in heaven and transform us, his children, here on earth. This transformation is meant to take place, not once or twice in a lifetime, but every time we worship, "with ever-increasing glory."

ULTIMATE WORSHIP

Surely God would not have created such a being as man...to exist only for a day! No, no, man was made for immortality.

ABRAHAM LINCOLN

Today I am one day nearer home than ever before. One day nearer the dawning when the fog will lift, mysteries clear, and all question marks straighten up into exclamation points! I shall see the King!

VANCE HAVNER

The life of heaven is the inexhaustible fountain of God's thought and God's love; how could it be boring?... Boredom, like pain, will be remembered only as a joke when we are "drenched in joy."

C. S. LEWIS

What can earth do for you if you are guaranteed heaven? To fear the worst earthly loss would be like a millionaire fearing the loss of a penny—less, a scratch on a penny.

PETER KREEFT

Eternity will not be long enough to learn all he is, or to praise him for all he has done, but then, that matters not, for we shall be always with him, and we desire nothing more.

FREDERICK WILLIAM FABER

16

WHY IS HEAVEN, HEAVEN?

No eye has seen,

no ear has heard,

no mind has conceived

what God has prepared for those who love him.

1 CORINTHIANS 2:9

When I was a brand new Christian, happy to be saved but an infant in the Scriptures, I was travelling in a car with some friends in northern Canada. As we drove and the day wore on, we came upon a vale of lush trees whose leaves were shaking in the wind. The sun was slowly going down, and as it did, the spectacle of light on leaves at sunset had an almost magical effect, as if each leaf had caught fire. It was breathtaking—everything a Van Gogh aspires to capture. There were "oohs" and "ahs" all around...you get the point.

At that very moment I heard these words—awful, feeble, milk-toasty words—so disappointing they fell like porridge to the ground. With a smile from ear to ear, the girl beside me gushed out, "I bet heaven is going to be ten times better than this!" Well, that was it. The plug was pulled and the music slowly died. I thought, *That's it? That's all? Ten times better? Why not a hundred times? Or a trillion? Or even a hundred trillion times better?* I was a coward though and said nothing.

WAY TOO SMALL

I hate so-called "cloud nine theology." I hate it because it damages the soul. (My friend in the car left the Lord years ago.) But what I hate, God must surely despise—those puny, childish pictures of heaven: Peter at the pearly gates, scroll in hand...endless white walls and fluffy clouds...harps and halos...fishing on tropical beaches...perfect golf games, and so on. People hear such descriptions and ask questions like, "What else will there be to do?"—as if boredom were even a remote possibility in the life to come. This is a fitting heaven for ants—for dogs, maybe—but certainly not for sons and daughters of God! Heaven is our one hope, our one longing, our whole reason for being. It is the goal and final redemption of all creation. It is the very end of the very beginning of all things. We need to grow up in our thinking, some of us desperately so.

Your heaven is too small. Mine is too small. If all of us together tried to outdo one another with wilder, bolder and more outrageous thoughts of heaven—we would still fall short. In fact, a whole mountain of wonderful thoughts, gathered together and lifted up, would not suffice. This exercise would leave us exhausted and happy, to be sure; but we would look up from that summit of superlatives only to realize that we had not yet begun to ascend the real peak, still towering hundreds of miles into the sky before us.

Ten times more? One hundred trillion times more? How about *infinitely* more? Heaven is infinitely more than our best, most wonderful and most outrageously creative thoughts. What, after all, do Biblical expressions like these tell us: "unsearchable," "immeasurable," "indescribable" and "inexpressible"? In heaven, we will dwell in the kingdom of an infinite God. We will enter into and become part of God's very own life—his abundant, eternal, creative, life-giving life. Mortality and every other limitation of this creation will be swallowed up by the life of the Eternal One.

So why try to imagine it at all? Because we are encouraged to do so again and again, even commanded to. You see, thoughts of heaven elevate us. They purify us (1 John 3:3), releasing us from the grip of this world (Colossians 3:1-4). They give us hope and endurance. They fill us with "inexpressible and glorious joy" (1 Peter 1:8). And besides, it's just plain fun!

TRUTH AND THE TASTE OF SHADOWS

Although we cannot truly imagine what heaven will be like—(Can a blind man understand the color blue?)—God has nonetheless given us important clues to help us on our way. These truths, however, are no more than a whisper, a hint or a scent. They are just enough to make us yearn for what is to come.

The descriptions we read in the Bible concerning heaven are *true* but not *graspable*. Not unlike, say, the equation $E = mc^2$ or the word "cheered." First the equation: Energy equals mass times the speed of light squared. This is a true statement. It was true before Einstein and nuclear bombs. It was true during the days of Noah, though no one had articulated it yet. A bit of the power of that equation can be understood from what is released in a nuclear reaction. For instance, just 2.6 kilograms of uranium can become a fireball easily capable of destroying entire cities in one burst. Matter that weighs no more than a small dumbbell can produce an explosion equal to 60 million tons of TNT! On the other hand, that same bit of matter could, when channeled through a reactor, provide enough electricity to light up those same cities for years to come. Still, even in the case of a nuclear blast, only a small percentage of the latent power is unleashed. All that energy is locked up—frozen, so to speak—in matter. Cool, eh?

God created $E = mc^2$, not Albert Einstein. He was just the first human to correctly formulate it. However, I would bet not one scientist—including Mr. Einstein—fully grasped the awesome fire contained in that simple equation until the first atomic bomb was tested.

Now the word "cheer." Cheer is what we do when someone blows out the candles, scores a goal or gets a "B+" in mathematics or social studies. I recently read this clip in the paper:

> "None of 86 Aboard Hurt in Touchdown." The Associated Press, San Francisco. A Delta Airlines jet with 86 people on board made an emergency landing after its landing gear jammed, sliding along the runway in a shower of sparks and

> severely damaging a wing. Passengers *cheered* as the jet came to a halt. (emphasis mine)

In this instance, "cheered" takes on a whole new dimension, doesn't it? This is the "we're-alive-and-not-dead" kind of cheer, way more meaningful than all of the other examples put together.

Similarly, words like "glory," "all," "life," "seed," "power"—not to mention "God"—all the words the Bible uses to describe heaven—are pregnant with meaning. Each contains a concept that is real, but ungraspable. These words provide us a taste. They are but hints and shadows. Through them we have a *veiled* sense of heaven. We are aroused and awakened and delighted, but we only see with the eyes of our hearts, in our spirits, in a mirror, dimly.

How does one imagine, then, what is unimaginable? The apostle John said, "What we will be has not yet been made known" (1 John 3:2). Even that statement is a wonderful clue, because many things have been said about heaven, things so amazing, they are almost unbelievable. Yet even after such a rich revelation of things to come, much more remains "unknown."

Nevertheless God has enjoined us to "set [our] hope fully on the grace to be given [us] when Christ is revealed" (1 Peter 1:13). We are to "set [our] hearts on things above, where Christ is seated at the right hand of God" (Colossians 3:1). Indeed, we Christians have "tasted the goodness of the word of God and the *powers of the coming age*" (Hebrews 6:5, emphasis mine). Even now, every disciple is "seated with him in the heavenly realms" (Ephesians 2:4-7). In a sense, we smell the feast from a distance and we salivate, like one of Pavlov's dogs.

What sort of clues has God given us about the nature and glory of heaven? For one, heaven is the eternal purpose of God. His one ambition, his singular goal for the cosmos, the *raison d'être* of all creation, is heaven! This purpose had no beginning; it is as eternal as God himself is (Ephesians 3:11). This purpose is a part of God's very being, intrinsic to his nature as God. All that has been made—the angels, the demons, thrones and powers, things visible and invisible, the plentitude of life and law and mystery, the earth, the nations, the prophets and patriarchs, the very first man to the very last—all are just part of the preparation for God's eternal purpose, the ultimate goal of all things: heaven. Think about the extensive wedding preparations that lead up to that perfect moment between two lovers—the kiss and the proclamation "you are now husband and wife." Only this time, God himself will pronounce the blessing upon his son Jesus Christ and upon us, "the wife of the Lamb" (Revelation 21:9).

To accomplish God's eternal purpose, it cost God everything he had: his one and only Son. Heaven is not something God simply made or possesses, but something he purchased for us. Creating the heavens and the earth cost God a word, a divine fiat, a breath from his mouth. But to redeem his creation and glorify his elect is a different matter altogether. This cost God not *a* word, but *the* Word, the life of his only begotten Son, "the Lamb that was slain from the creation of the world" (Revelation 13:8; John 1:1-2).

What motivated Jesus to give his life? As awful as the sufferings of Christ were, unthinkably evil and horrible, the end result was clearly in his mind. What motivated the God-man to become "nothing" and die? It was for "the *joy* set before him" (Hebrews 12:2, emphasis mine). Something so wonderful will happen one day that Christ was willing to become sin for us (2 Corinthians 5:21), to be made nothing (Philippians 2:7), to be "cursed" by his Father (Galatians 3:13), to be slaughtered (Isaiah 53:7) and "forsaken" (Matthew 27:46). He did not die just "to rescue us from the present evil age" (Galatians 1:4), but in order to "[bring] many sons to glory" (Hebrews 2:10), to a place of unspeakable joy. Who can imagine a joy that far outweighs even the sufferings of Christ—a joy so glorious that the eternal, sinless, holy One of God actually became sin to accomplish it? His deep and profound sacrifice evokes thunderous praise in heaven even now (Revelation 5), and it will continue to do so throughout all eternity. In love, he gave all he had for "the joy set before him" (Hebrews 12:2). What is this joy? I believe it is we, the church.

THE WORLD IS NOT ENOUGH

Another hint about the nature of heaven can be found in the creation itself. This little planet is gushing with life. In the words of Elizabeth Barrett Browning, "Earth is crammed with heaven, and every common bush aflame with God." Men love to build things; but God is the architect of all that is and lives. He is all powerful, all wise, supremely creative.

Countless trillions of living organisms exist upon the earth. About two million species have been catalogued, with estimates that as many as two hundred million more remain to be discovered! Every shovelful of dirt is bristling with life—myriad species of organisms, each one stunningly complex, even beautiful. In fact, the physiology of just one termite is more complex than the nuclear fusion currently taking place in every star in the heavens. Right now, if you can believe it, several hundred scientists around the globe work full time to decipher the embryology and biomechanics of just one insect, the common fruit fly. One of them likens his research to the thrill of plundering King Tut's tomb: uncovering rooms and layers and mysteries and gold, then deeper still, until finally—voila—Tutankhamun![1] You've gotta love these guys.

What can the starry skies teach us about heaven? Just a few years ago it was estimated that there are 10^{21} stars out there. That's 1,000,000,000,000,000,000,000 stars. How big is that number? If we could somehow reduce each of these stars to the size of a grain of sand, there would be enough to cover the continental United States with a layer of sand twelve inches deep. Today, however, scientists tell us there are more stars than grains of sand in the whole world. In fact, who's even counting anymore? Billions of light-years in all directions (one light-year equals about six trillion miles), the known universe is dotted with galaxies, each one a cluster of billions and even trillions of individual stars—some of which are hundreds of times larger, thousands of times more massive, and millions of times brighter than our own sun.

---

[1] Peter A. Lawrence, *The Making of a Fly* (Oxford, UK: Blackwell Sciences Ltd, 1992), xi.

More remarkable still, as our knowledge of the universe expands, almost exponentially, the universe itself is expanding as "billions upon billions of cubic light years of space [are] added to the volume of the universe *every second*."[2] The boundary of the known universe is receding from us at rates approaching 70-80% of the speed of light!

Amazingly, with all these gazillions of stars, we still must call it "space." For in spite of the countless number of objects out there, the distances between stars are vast, making most of the visible universe seem empty. For example, the closest star to us, Proxima Centauri, is about 4.2 light-years away. Think of it, our *closest* stellar neighbor is twenty-five trillion miles away.[3] God created all of this space and all of these stars with only a word from his mouth. Every last one is special and has a unique name and a unique splendor (1 Corinthians 15:41). Each is exactly where God wants it to be.

Truly, "the heavens declare the glory of God" (Psalm 19:1)! They bear witness to his "eternal power and divine nature" (Romans 1:20). Nevertheless, the heavens are "reserved for fire" (2 Peter 3:7). God will set them aside as easily as taking off a garment or blowing out a candle (Psalm 102:25-27). Who can begin to conceive, therefore, what "the powers of the coming age" (Hebrews 6:5) might be? What does God have in store for us in paradise? If these heavens are but the fringes of his power, a faint whisper, what of the fullness of his power to be revealed in the "new heavens" (Isaiah 65:17)?

TONGUE-TIED

Heaven is beyond language. Paul made reference to "inexpressible things" (2 Corinthians 12:4) and things that "no ear has heard" (1 Corinthians 2:9). This too is a wonderful clue. Not that language doesn't apply, but language is not enough. If we plundered and pillaged every dictionary and every thesaurus in every language, piling word upon word, it still would not be enough. Heaven is beyond language, because God is beyond language. Even when we shall be in heaven

---

[2] John Archibald Wheeler, *A Journey into Gravity and Spacetime*, Scientific American Library, (New York: W. H. Freeman Company, 1990), 2.

[3] If our sun were shrunk to the size of a dot over the letter "i" and so was Proxima Centauri, they would be about ten miles apart!

itself, words will not be enough to describe he who is unsearchable and immeasurable, higher than "the highest heavens" (2 Chronicles 6:18).

What did the apostle John experience along these lines? By the time he had recorded the first twenty chapters of the book of Revelation, John was already on tiptoe, stretched to the capacity of human imagination. Then he was transported even higher, by an angel, to a tall mountain (Revelation 21:10). Caught up by the Spirit, he saw farther than any man has ever seen; but he had not seen it all. Coming down from higher still, from heaven, was the New Jerusalem, the city of God. The vision he received of heaven was so overwhelming that he fell down to worship at the feet of the angel who merely showed him those things. (That's a no-no.) He did it twice! (See Revelation 19:10, 22:8.) John knew better (1 John 5:21), but he just couldn't help himself. A simple vision, by a mere angel—not the realities themselves—and he fell face down to worship.

What about Paul? Paul was "caught up to the third heaven" to "paradise," and heard "inexpressible things, things that man is not permitted to tell" (2 Corinthians 12:1-10). So disoriented was he by the grandeur of his revelation, he wasn't even sure if he was in his body or not. What did he see? Something so wonderful, so surpassingly, exceedingly wonderful, that God gave him a thorn in the flesh *for the rest of his life*, a "messenger of Satan," to keep him from becoming conceited because of these visions.

Paul's desire for heaven, his wish "to depart and be with Christ" (Philippians 1:23), pushed and pulled him to the limits of sacrifice and suffering and shame. And yet, what does the scarred, beaten and broken man have to say about his life? "Our present sufferings are not worth comparing with the glory that will be revealed in us" (Romans 8:18). And again, "our light and momentary troubles are achieving for us an eternal glory that far outweighs them all" (2 Corinthians 4:17).

The experiences of these two men offer more clues, the taste of shadows. Their earnest words, simple gestures and passing statements contain remarkable, stunning truths.

And so we come nearer to our main point: Why is heaven, heaven? In heaven, Paul says, we shall be "swallowed up in life" (2 Corinthians 5:4).

That even sounds good, doesn't it? Inhaled, swallowed, enveloped and invaded by life itself, life that springs from the source of all life, from the architect of living things, from the eternal life himself.

We will inherit from God—catch your breath—"all things" (Romans 8:32). Everything that God's mind can imagine, that his power can accomplish, that his love can lavish, shall be given to us. We are his offspring, true sons and daughters with the legal rights of heirs. We own "the whole estate" (Galatians 4:1). We have the right to eat in the paradise of God (Revelation 2:7). When the Bible says "all things," it means "all things." And why should it not? As we have said previously, if God "did not spare his own Son but gave him up for us all—how will he not also, along with him, graciously give us all things?" (Romans 8:32). Still...this is not why heaven is heaven.

WORLDLY WONDERS

More clues are to be found in this physical universe, whose purpose is to reveal God and to be good to man. What is here is not God's glory, but it declares his glory, his invisible qualities, his divine nature and his eternal power (Romans 1:20). This world is a sort of "Look what I can do," a kind of "lay[ing] bare of my holy arm" (Isaiah 52:10). It is full of splendid artifacts, shadows, bits and pieces of things in the realm of space and time. When our own shadows are projected onto a wall, they say *something* about us. What they say is truthful, but limited; in the end they are only 2-D moving outlines—not even the remotest picture of our real glory. The whole of creation is but the shadow of God!

God is the awesome designer of every life form, including some that we may find humorous, like the platypus and the ostrich. He is the God of my senses, my imagination and my personality. He invented the whole vast particle zoo of the nuclear world—quarks, leptons, bosons and the elusive Higgs particle—"the God particle." He is the architect of cosmic string, if such a thing exists—whether in ten or twenty-six dimensions. He has given us quantum mechanics, special relativity, the curvature of space-time, the mysteries of light-speed and the spooky phenomenon of particle-wave duality. He has made possible the almost infinite material possibilities from just three building blocks: neutrons, protons and electrons. He is the architect who devised DNA, the human seed, a world gushing with life and wonders, stars that declare his glory day after day, and deep secrets that are begging to be discovered—"the glory of kings" (Proverbs 25:2). God devised geometry and patterns, orbits and ellipses, tastes and smells and colors and textures, and the fundamental forces of gravity, electricity, and the strong and weak nuclear forces. He is the God of proteins and enzymes, frost and fluid dynamics, chaos and symmetry, ocean vents and ovulation, fractal geometry and fingerprints, phyllotaxis and the Fibonacci sequence, the *spira mirabalis* and Leonardo da Vinci's *sectio divina*.

His mind conceived neural anatomy. He is the God of my brain—"the three-pound universe"—its pumps and volts and gates, its charges and salts, carriers and crossings, signals and symmetries, and the chemical and electrical symphonies of hundreds of trillions of synapses. He fashioned the heart and hemoglobin, mitosis and meiosis. God engineered snowflakes and lightning, silkworms and bombardier beetles, the gentle effects of gravity on growth and form. He is behind the parabola of a high fly at a baseball game, the circular wake made by a pebble in a quiet pond and the mathematical perfection of a sunflower, the laws of thermodynamics and the motion of heavenly spheres, black holes and pulsars, rainbows and daydreams. He is the conductor of the ballet of courtship and sexual chemistry—not only of man, but of everything on earth.

God is the author of Kepler's ellipticals, Maxwell's equations, Newton's laws, Mendeleyev's periodic table and Einstein's relativities; Galileo's moons, Reinman's geometry, Lorenzo's transformations, Heisenberg's uncertainty and Pauli's exclusion; Bohm's implicate order, Schrödinger's matter waves, Hawking's singularities, Hubble's red shift and Planck's constant.

Amazingly, all of this—the whole shebang—is for man, a gift to him. God has designed a suitable habitation just for us, for men and women created in his image. Earth is a place where God is near enough so that men are without excuse, and yet hidden enough so that we must search for him. Nevertheless all laws and life-forms, love and lovemaking—all are for man. And they are especially meant for the few, the chosen, the elect of God.

This planet is our home, our arena, or in the words of John Keats, our "vale of soul making." It is the stage of God's eternal drama, and it is *very* good (Genesis 1:31). But it shall perish when God declares, "I am making everything new!" (Revelation 21:5). Paul declared, "The creation itself will be liberated from its bondage to decay and brought into the glorious freedom of the children of God" (Romans 8:21).

We must pause here to ask: If earth is intended as a worthy home for mankind, what must God's own home be like? We have been called "into his kingdom and glory" (1 Thessalonians 2:12) and we will one day step into the very home of God, who is the "architect and builder" of better things (Hebrews 11:10).

THE BODY HUMAN

God is the God of the human form, "fearfully and wonderfully made" (Psalm 139:14). Indeed, the body he has created is so miraculous, so wonderful and amazing, that it has been described in countless millions of words in hundreds of medical libraries. So much research has been done by scientists the world over, and yet we have barely scratched the surface of understanding one human cell, let alone the whole body. We don't even know how a single protein or a solitary enzyme really works.

At the moment of conception, one human egg is so unimaginably complex and orderly that almost every textbook written on the subject uses the word "miraculous." The process of uniting a sperm and an egg, their unique and original genetic codes converging into one, surpasses the complexity of two civilizations being joined together in the blink of an eye. It would be as though Moscow and New York were instantly meshed together, and all of their plumbing and wiring worked in concert, their computers never crashed, their citizens could understand each other's languages, and the bureaucrats instantly became best friends!

Look at what God is able to do with that one human seed. In a mere nine months, a human seed—an egg and a sperm—will grow hundreds of trillions of times as large as its original self. It will have a body to experience the world and both a soul and spirit with which to discover itself and reach out to God. When born, it enters a vast universe of color and sound, taste and touch. It reasons, loves, procreates and can (if it wants to) figure out equations like $E = mc^2$, create sonnets and symphonies, or even have a burping contest. It is able to reach out and comprehend stuff that is billions of light-years away and, remarkably, find its place in this universe. A speck, no bigger than a pinprick, grasping the fringes of the universe, can look up and actually find God! But even more: that little seed has the potential to become the bride of Christ—now that, my friends, is a good egg.

John declared that God's seed is in us (1 John 3:9). We know that seeds bear fruit according to their kind (Genesis 1:11). If that is what God can do with one *human* seed, what are we destined to become with *God's* seed in us? Prepare to be like God!

THE BODY IMMORTAL

In heaven we will be given new bodies—glorified, exalted, immortal, spiritual bodies. With these bodies will come unimaginable powers to comprehend and communicate because of God's life flowing through us. We will be equipped to withstand the adventures, discoveries and wonders of heaven without exploding in joy or being consumed by glory. Our bodies will be just "like his glorious body" (Philippians 3:21). And just as we have borne the likeness of Adam, the man from earth, "so shall we bear the likeness of the man from heaven" (1 Corinthians 15:49). For his life and nature have been imparted to us. This is no delusion of grandeur. We are born of God, born of his Spirit, and partakers of the divine nature.

Moreover, heaven will be a country of Christlike beings. How wonderful! God's plan is to bring "many sons to glory" (Hebrews 2:10). Each and every one of us will be glorified, perfect and full to overflowing with divine love. Every interaction will be a blessing; every word, a gracious word; every exchange, a gift. Every action and every thought will be kind, beautiful, holy and pure. We will never again sin against each other—it will not cross our minds. There will be no temptation, nothing whatsoever to harm us. We will love each other as deeply as Christ himself, as God himself loves us.

We will serve our God and each other without tiring. I suppose we will inhale and exhale the love of Christ even as we do oxygen now. Each of us will be like Christ, who was "the firstborn among many brothers" (Romans 8:29) but also, each of us will enjoy a spectacular uniqueness. This profound specialness, I believe, will be God's way of completing and perfecting the fellowship of the saints. Like lock and key, we will truly need each other in the highest possible sense. No wonder it is called "a better country" (Hebrews 11:16).

We will be glorified to the highest possible degree. This is the privilege and final goal of our redemption. "And those he predestined, he also called; those he called, he also justified; those he justified, he also glorified" (Romans 8:30). God will exalt us to a place so high, to a height so unimaginable, that it is not possible to be exalted any further without breaching the Godhead. Through Christ the God-man, we will share not *a* glory but *his* glory (John 17:24). Into "his kingdom and glory" we are called (1 Thessalonians 2:12).

Who will be in heaven? Only the redeemed and angels? Have you ever considered there may be countless numbers of other spiritual life forms with us as well? What about all the "rulers and authorities in the heavenly realms" (Ephesians 3:10)? What about the millions and millions of children who have died in birth or abortion or in their innocence? Perhaps all of the living things from this creation will share in the redemption and be freed from their bondage (Romans 8:21). If God can turn a chunk of coal into a diamond by the slight shift of carbon atoms, maybe that ugly spider will become a fireworks display in paradise!

SHARING GOD'S HOME

> He who was seated on the throne said, "I am making everything new!" Then he said, "Write this down, for these words are trustworthy and true." (Revelation 21:5)

All things will be new: new colors, new sounds, new everything. A friend once said to me, "the only man-made thing in heaven will be the nail marks in Jesus' hands." In heaven, we will discover the depths of *all* the wisdom and treasures of God's mind and heart (Colossians 2:2-3). We will be shown the glories and incomparable vastness of his creative imagination—maybe even enter it, as in a dream. Perhaps we will be given new creative powers ourselves—powers to compose, to build, or to set out on voyages of discovery—powers worthy of true sons of God. What awaits us is surprise upon surprise, wonder upon wonder, treasure upon treasure, splendor upon splendor. Every moment will be like having our eyes opened for the very first time. We will experience unfading powers, riches, adventures, pleasures and feasts. Secrets will be uncovered, laws understood, questions answered, mysteries made known. We will *never* say, "What else is there to do here?" The glory will never diminish, never bore us even for a moment. Even as the members of the trinity are satisfied within themselves, so shall we be, for it is their life that will course through us. A man was once asked, "What's the first thing you're going to do when you get to heaven?" and he answered, "For the first thousand years, I'm just gonna stand around and grin." Amen to that!

In heaven, we will enjoy not the paradise of man but of God. What is God's own home like, the place where the fullness of his glory dwells? After all, he is the God of all beauty and splendor, all light and mystery.

Heaven is the home of the spirits of righteous men made perfect. It is a place of unutterable moral perfection. Heaven is the Holy of Holies, the dwelling place of God. The tabernacle of Moses' day and the temple of Solomon each contained a small room (30 x 30 x 30 feet), a cube, that was called the Holy of Holies. There is another cube mentioned in Scripture, in the book of Revelation, the only other cube mentioned in the Bible. It is the city of God, and its dimensions are about fifteen hundred miles by fifteen hundred miles by fifteen hundred miles. This is the dwelling place of God—not the Holy of Holies on earth, but the Holy of Holies in heaven itself. The intended impact of John's vision is clear—heaven is exponential in holiness, exponential in glory, exponential in Presence. What is his home like, the place where his glory dwells? It is into this paradise that God welcomes us.

We could go on and on and on. And yet, as wonderful, mysterious and "unbelievable" as these blessings seem, they are not ultimately what make heaven, heaven. They are only a part of it. Even our glorification is only a part of it, a means to an end. And what is that end? It is nothing short of God himself. He is the Beginning, and *he* is the End.

GOD WITH MAN

So why is heaven, heaven? Because finally, for the first time in all eternity, we will see the face of God in full disclosure. No one has ever seen the fullness of God's glory except for Christ (John 1:18)—not even the angels. Angels, of course, see his face; they "stand in the presence of God" (Luke 1:19). But they are not capable of beholding his fullness for they are not created in the image of God. They are to God as the animals were to Adam, creatures but not the counterpart. Adam could only deeply fellowship with one just like himself, from himself, his Eve. When we see God, this will be the first full disclosure of God in all of eternity. We will see who God really is. We will behold how wonderful God really is. We will come to understand how loving God really is. This blessing is reserved only for the elect, the special few, the called, chosen and faithful, the bride of his Son. Finally we shall come face to face with our Creator, our Redeemer, our "Father who art in heaven." God has reserved this moment from all eternity for us, just for us, and only for us. It will be the special and sacred revelation and sacred beginning to an eternal honeymoon with Christ. "The two shall become one flesh." This is a profound mystery, declares Paul, "but I am talking about Christ and the church" (Ephesians 5:31-32). "We shall be like him, for we shall see him as he is" (1 John 3:2).

In heaven, we are welcomed into the fullness of the love of the Father, the Son and the Holy Spirit. We will be brought into the fellowship of the Godhead. Because we are adopted, we will be glorified and we will reign with Christ. We will fully share in the love that the trinity has exchanged among themselves from before creation. As Eve was to Adam, bone of his bone and flesh of his flesh, so we are to Christ. Truly, "this is a profound mystery"! (See Ephesians 5:32.)

Believe the unbelievable, receive the inconceivable: We will *see* God. We have been created for this one purpose: to be cups and mirrors, as it were, to hold and reflect the contents of God's glory. What theologians call the beatific vision, I call flat awesome! Adam could not have true fellowship with animals because they were not like him; they could not have intimate exchanges because they were not "bone of [his] bones" (Genesis 2:23). To have the deepest possible fellowship with God, we must be like him. And that, my brothers and sisters, is who we are: bone from his bone, flesh from his flesh, life from his life, love from his love, glory from his glory.

I'M NOT WORTHY

"Why God, why?" I dare not speak for God; but as I ponder these mysteries, it seems to me that *God is so wonderful that he must be shared.* Just as Eve—something outside of Adam but like Adam—came from Adam, God created a plan whereby humankind—something outside of himself, but from himself—would be able to seek him and find him and love him in return, and finally to be lifted up to become like God. Creature from Creator—but *glorified* creature—that we might look upon God and enjoy him forever. As Eve looked to Adam, so shall we look to Christ, the last Adam, our beloved, and to our heavenly Father. Just as Adam and Eve were to exercise dominion over all the earth, we too, as Christ's bride, shall reign with him on his throne to exercise dominion and authority in the heavenly realms. We shall rule and reign with him as his co-heir, co-sovereign and full counterpart in paradise.

> Then I heard what sounded like a great multitude, like the roar of rushing waters and like loud peals of thunder, shouting:
>
> "Hallelujah!
>   For our Lord God Almighty reigns.
>   Let us rejoice and be glad
>   and give him glory!

> For the wedding of the Lamb has come,
> and his bride has made herself ready."
> (Revelation 19:6-7)

We shall enjoy everything God is capable of giving to us. This is the ultimate and final disclosure of God. All that God is, has and desires shall be made known to us—especially his love.

APPENDIX

HOW DO I LOVE THEE?

E lizabeth Barrett Browning was a woman in love, deeply in love. Very few of us have never heard the line, "How do I love thee? Let me count the ways." Not as many know the rest of this great poem, written to her husband. Not only her expressions, but the public declaration of such love is quite beautiful. Mrs. Browning's emotions ran free like wild horses and human language could barely rein them in.

The Psalms are Hebrew poetry, inspired by the Holy Spirit. They are a treasure house of emotion and verbal expression, bright or dark. It seems every emotion that can be emoted is found in the book of Psalms. This extreme range of emotions expressed is perhaps best summarized in Psalm 88 and Psalm 89. Heman the Ezrahite ends Psalm 88 with these words:

> But I cry to you for help, O LORD;
>   in the morning my prayer comes before you.
> Why, O LORD, do you reject me
>   and hide your face from me?
> From my youth I have been afflicted and close to death;
>   I have suffered your terrors and am in despair.
> Your wrath has swept over me;
>   your terrors have destroyed me.
> All day long they surround me like a flood;
>   they have completely engulfed me.
> You have taken my companions and loved ones from me;
>   the darkness is my closest friend. (Psalm 88:13-18)

But in contrast, Ethan the Ezrahite (a cousin or a brother or family member?) begins Psalm 89 like this:

I will sing of the Lord's great love forever;
>   with my mouth I will make your faithfulness known
>   through all generations.
I will declare that your love stands firm forever,
>   that you established your faithfulness in heaven itself.

You said, "I have made a covenant with my chosen one,
>   I have sworn to David my servant,
'I will establish your line forever
>   and make your throne firm through all generations.'"
(Psalm 89:1-4)

In order for us to understand all the different aspects of worship and the depth of feeling associated with them, consider the following different descriptions of worship. But again, the emphasis here is on *personal* worship. Worship is extremely personal. He is *my* light, *my* salvation, I pour out *my* soul, etc. And again,

My lips will shout for joy
>   when I sing praise to you —
>   I, whom you have redeemed. (Psalm 71:23)

Consider the wide array of emotions, postures, and gestures, attitudes and actions that are expressed throughout the Scriptures regarding the worship of our amazing God. Take time in your private worship to read the following verses.

I lift (Psalm 20:5, 24:7, 25:1)
I declare (Psalm 22:22, 75:9, 89:2, 106:2; 1 Peter 2:9; Isaiah 12:4-6)
I seek (Psalm 27, 77:1-2)
I call (Psalm 28:1)
I depend (Psalm 63:7-8)
I ascribe (Psalm 29)
I exalt (Psalm 30:1, 40:16, 89:16, 99:5, 145:1; Isaiah 24:14-16, 25:1)
I acknowledge (Psalm 30)
I trust (Psalm 31:14-15, 56:3-4)
I extol (Psalm 109:30, 111:1)

I boast (Psalm 34:1-2, 44:8, 92:5)

I delight (Psalm 37:4; Isaiah 61:10)

I recount (Psalm 40:5, 74:13-17)

I desire (Psalm 40:6-8)

I pant (Psalm 42:1)

I thirst (Psalm 42:1, 63:1; Jeremiah 2:13)

I pour (Psalm 42:4)

I cast (Psalm 55:22)

I awaken (Psalm 57:8)

I sing (Psalm 59:16-17)

I long (Psalm 63:1-2)

I laugh (Psalm 126:2)

I overflow (Psalm 119:171)

I live (Psalm 119:175, 142:7)

I ponder (Psalm 111, 147)

I wait (Psalm 130:6)

I dance (Psalm 149:3)

I sit (1 Chronicles 17:16-22)

I pray (Psalm 141:2)

I celebrate (Psalm 145:7)

I shout (Psalm 81:1, 95:1)

I meditate (Psalm 77:12)

I rest (Psalm 62:1-2, 5-7)

I behold (Psalm 63:2)

I remember (Psalm 63:6, 78:11, 111:2-4, 143:5-6)

I proclaim (Psalm 68:34-35)

I glorify (Psalm 63:3, 69:30)

I tell (Psalm 71:15, 73:28, 78:3-6, 107:22)

I vow (Psalm 76:11)

I appeal (Psalm 77:10-11, 132:2)

I dwell (Psalm 90:1)

I kneel (Psalm 95:6-7)

I glory (Psalm 106:47; Isaiah 41:16)

I thank (Psalm 100:4, 116:17)
I treasure (Psalm 119:72)
I tremble (Psalm 114:7; Isaiah 66:2)
I fall (Revelation 4:10-11)
I participate (1 Corinthians 10:16)
I yearn (Isaiah 26:8-9)

All these depths of responses and feelings need to fill our hearts as we worship God. When we truly worship God and pour out our hearts and lift up our souls, and call from the depths, and spread out our hands, and celebrate with all our might, and dance and kneel before our maker, and gaze and gaze and gaze upon the beauty and light and splendor of God, he is glorified and we are satisfied. Whoever said the church is boring? The church is where the action is!

WHO ARE WE?

Discipleship Publications International (DPI) began publishing in 1993. We are a nonprofit Christian publisher affiliated with the International Churches of Christ, committed to publishing and distributing materials that honor God, lift up Jesus Christ and show how his message practically applies to all areas of life. We have a deep conviction that no one changes life like Jesus and that the implementation of his teaching will revolutionize any life, any marriage, any family and any singles household.

Since our beginning, we have published more than 100 titles; plus, we have produced a number of important, spiritual audio products. More than one million volumes have been printed, and our works have been translated into more than a dozen languages—international is not just a part of our name! Our books are shipped regularly to every inhabited continent.

To see a more detailed description of our works, find us on the World Wide Web at www.dpibooks.org. You can order books by calling 1-888-DPI-BOOK twenty-four hours a day. From outside the US, call 781-937-3883, ext. 231 during Boston-area business hours.

We appreciate the hundreds of comments we have received from readers. We would love to hear from you. Here are other ways to get in touch:

Mail: DPI, One Merrill St., Woburn, MA 01801
E-Mail: dpibooks@icoc.org

FIND US ON THE
WORLD WIDE WEB

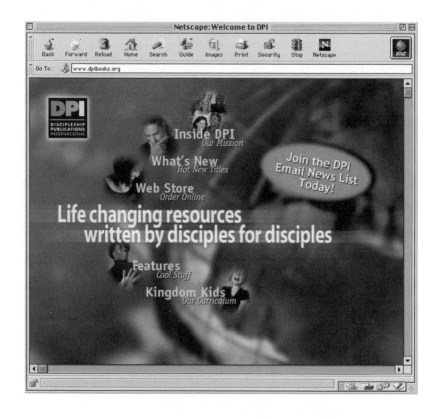

WWW.DPIBOOKS.ORG

1-888-DPI-BOOK

OUTSIDE US: 781-937-3883 x231